101 Foundation-Pieced
Quilt Blocks

by Linda Causee

Bobbie Matela, Managing Editor
Carol Wilson Mansfield, Art Director
Meredith Montross, Associate Editor
Christina Wilson, Assistant Editor
Graphic Solutions inc-chgo, Book Design

For a full-color catalog including books on
quilting, write to:

American School of Needlework®
Consumer Division
1455 Linda Vista Drive
San Marcos, CA 92069

**Photographed blocks stitched by Linda Causee, Candy Matthews,
Meredith Montross, and Christina Wilson**

©1996 by American School of Needlework®, Inc.; ASN Publishing, 1455 Linda Vista Drive, San Marcos, CA 92069

Introduction

It has been wonderful to watch this collection of foundation blocks start as just a pile of black and white drawings and come to life with colorful fabrics. Everyone on our staff loves new and unusual quilt blocks. It's great fun to plan new quilts using these new blocks along with some tried and true favorites. All blocks are a 7"-square finished size so they can be combined easily when you plan your own full-sized quilt or wallhanging.

Linda Causee of our staff has designed some intricate blocks that are easy to do using foundation piecing methods. If you've never tried foundation piecing you're in for a real treat. Patchwork pieces are added to a foundation using a stitch-and-flip-open technique. This eliminates timely matching of points and seams.

Linda had such fun designing these blocks we think she could have done over a thousand—but we had to stop her and choose our favorite **101 Foundation-Pieced Quilt Blocks**. She has also included instructions for planning and finishing your own original quilt using these 7" blocks. We hope this collection of blocks becomes a treasured part of your quilting library.

Foundation Piecing is the technique of sewing patchwork onto a foundation such as paper or fabric following a numerical sequence. The stitching lines are drawn on the foundation. The fabric is placed on the unmarked (right) side while being sewn on the marked (wrong) side. Foundation piecing allows the quilter to piece even the tiniest pieces more accurately since all sewing will follow drawn lines. This technique can be done by either hand or machine, so you can take your blocks with you and stitch wherever you go.

Foundation Material

First, you must decide what type of foundation to use for piecing your blocks. There are several options. A light-colored, lightweight cotton fabric or muslin are popular choices. A lightweight fabric will be light enough to see through to trace onto and will give extra stability to your blocks. Of course, it will add another layer of fabric which you will have to quilt through. This extra thickness is a consideration only if you plan to do hand quilting. Another choice for foundations is paper. Use any paper that you can see through (notebook paper, copy paper, newsprint, or computer paper) for easy tracing, then tear it away after sewing is completed. A third choice is Tear Away® interfacing. Like muslin, it is light enough to see through for tracing, but like paper, it can later be easily removed for quilting.

Mirror Images

Many of the blocks in this collection are not symmetrical and will therefore produce a mirror image of the block pattern, **Fig 1**. On each pattern page (pages 12 to 116), there is a small diagram showing how the block will look once it has been pieced. Note however that the block diagram doesn't necessarily match fabric choices of the completed blocks shown photographed on the front and back covers and pages 49 to 52.

Fig 1   **Block #28**

Preparing the Foundation

Tracing the Block

Trace the block pattern carefully onto your chosen foundation material. Use a ruler and a fine-point permanent marker to make straight lines and be sure to include all numbers. Draw a line ¼" from the outside edges of the block, **Fig 2**; cut along outside drawn line. Repeat for the needed number of blocks for your quilt. If the block pattern you are tracing is not symmetrical, the completed block will be the mirror image of the pattern.

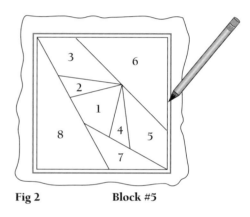

Fig 2   **Block #5**

*Hint: If you want a block to look like the pattern (for example, if you want Sunbonnet Sue to face left as it appears on page 43), you must first trace onto tracing paper, then flop pattern and trace onto foundation material, **Fig 3**.*

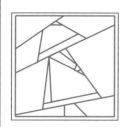 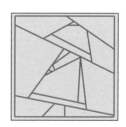 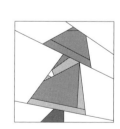

Fig 3 - Block #32   **Flop and Trace onto Foundation**

Transferring the Block

The block patterns can also be transferred onto foundation material using a transfer pen or pencil. Trace the block pattern onto paper using a transfer pen or pencil. Then following manufacturer's directions, iron transfer onto foundation material. Write numbers on foundation using a fine-point permanent marking pen. The block, if not symmetrical, will look like the pattern as it appears in the book, but will be a mirror image to the completed block shown in the color photographs. For example, if you trace the Sunbonnet Sue pattern (in the example above) onto paper and then **transfer** onto a foundation, it will face to the left.

Hint: If you want your unsymmetrical block to look like the completed block shown in color and you are using a transfer pen or pencil (for example, if you want Sunbonnet to face right), transfer as described above. But, if you would like your Sunbonnet Sue to face left, you must trace first with a permanent pen onto tracing paper, flop the design and trace again with the transfer pen or pencil.

Fabric

Unless you want special effects for your blocks such as a shiny satin Christmas Ornament (block #80), use 100% cotton fabric for the blocks. By using cotton rather than cotton/polyester, the pieces will stay in place easier after finger pressing. When using a fabric other than cotton, be sure to pin or glue the piece in place after each step.

Pre-washing fabric is not necessary, but it is necessary to test your fabric to make certain that the fabric is colorfast and preshrunk (don't trust those manufacturer's labels). Start by cutting a 2"-wide strip (cut crosswise) of each of the fabrics that you have selected for your quilt. To determine whether the fabric is colorfast, put each strip separately into a clean bowl of extremely hot water, or hold the fabric strip under hot running water. If your fabric bleeds a great deal, all is not necessarily lost. It might only be necessary to wash all of that fabric until all of the excess dye has washed out. Fabrics which continue to bleed after they have been washed several times should be eliminated.

To test for shrinkage, take each saturated strip and iron it dry with a hot iron. When the strip is completely dry, measure and compare it to your original measurements. If all of your fabric strips shrink about the same amount, then you really have no problem. When you wash your finished quilt, you may achieve the puckered look of an antique quilt. If you do not want this look, you will have to wash and dry all of the fabric before beginning so that shrinkage is no longer a problem. If only one of your fabrics is shrinking more than the others, it will have to be washed and dried, or discarded.

Cutting the Fabric

The beauty of foundation piecing is that you do **NOT** have to cut every exact piece for every block. You can use strips, rectangles, squares or any odd-shaped scrap for piecing. You **DO** have to be careful to use a piece of fabric that is at least ¼" larger on all sides than the space it is to cover. Triangle shapes can be a little tricky to piece. Use generous-sized fabric pieces and be careful when positioning the pieces onto the foundation. You do waste some fabric this way, but the time it saves in cutting will be worth it in the end.

Foundation Piecing

1. Prepare foundations as described in Preparing the Foundation, page 4.

2. Turn foundation with unmarked side facing you and position fabric piece 1 over the space marked 1 on the foundation. Hold foundation up to a light source to make sure that fabric overlaps at least ¼" on all sides of space 1; pin or glue in place with a glue stick, **Fig 4**.

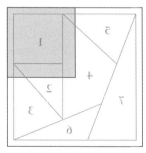

Fig 4   **Block #76**

3. Place fabric piece 2 right sides together with piece 1. *Note: Double check to see if fabric piece chosen will cover space 2 completely by folding over along line between space 1 and 2, Fig 5*.

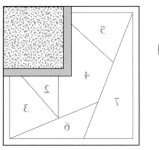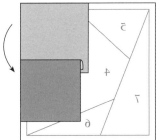

Fig 5

4. Turn foundation with **marked** side facing you and fold foundation forward along line between spaces 1 and 2; trim both pieces about 1/4" above fold line, **Fig 6**.

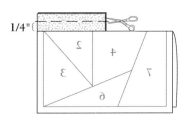

Fig 6

5. With marked side of foundation still facing you and using a very small stitch (to allow for easier paper removal), sew along line between spaces 1 and 2, **Fig 7**; begin and end two to three stitches beyond line.

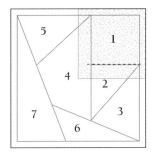

Fig 7

6. Turn foundation over. Open piece 2 and finger press seam, **Fig 8**. Use a pin or glue stick to hold piece in place.

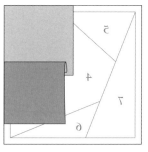

Fig 8

7. Turn foundation with **marked side** facing you; fold foundation forward along line between spaces 2 and 3 and trim piece 2 about 1/4" from fold, **Fig 9**.

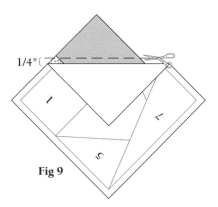

Fig 9

8. Place fabric 3 right side down even with just-trimmed edge, **Fig 10**.

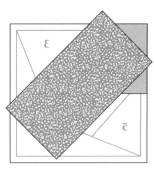

Fig 10

6

9. Turn foundation to marked side and sew along line between spaces 2 and 3; begin and end sewing 2 or 3 stitches beyond line, **Fig 11**.

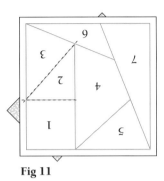

Fig 11

10. Turn foundation over, open piece 3 and finger press seam, **Fig 12**. Glue or pin in place.

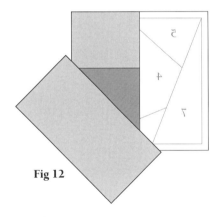

Fig 12

11. Turn foundation with **marked** side facing you; fold foundation forward along line between spaces 1, 2 and 4. If previous stitching makes it difficult to fold foundation forward, pull paper foundation away from fabric at stitching, then fold along line. If using a fabric foundation, fold it forward as far as it will go and trim to about 1/4" from drawn line, **Fig 13**.

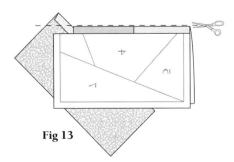

Fig 13

12. Continue trimming and sewing pieces in numerical order until block is complete. Press block, then trim fabric even with outside line of foundation, **Fig 14**, to complete block, **Fig 15**. Do not remove paper or Tear Away® at this time. It will stabilize the blocks when sewing them together since grainline was not considered and many of the edges of the blocks can be stretchy, bias edges.

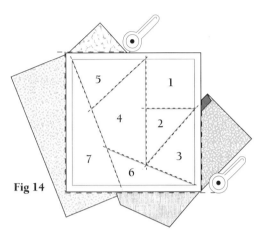

Fig 14

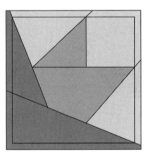

Fig 15

Planning a Quilt

Determine the size quilt you are making using the following chart as a guide.

Bed Size	Mattress Size
Crib	27" x 51"
Twin	39" x 75"
Double	54" x 75"
Queen	60" x 80"
King	76" x 80"

To the mattress size, add the drop (the part of the quilt that hangs over the edge of the mattress) and tuck (the part that is tucked under the pillows). For example, if you want your quilt to hang 12" over the edge of the mattress with a 12" tuck, add 24" to the length and width of the mattress size.

The blocks in this book all have a finished size of 7" square. Therefore, you can use any of the blocks in your quilt and they will fit together. Combine sashing and borders with the blocks to achieve the desired size. For example, a twin size quilt, **Quilt Layout 1**, with a finished size of 63" x 99" could be made with 60 blocks set six across and ten down with 2" sashing and a 3½" border.

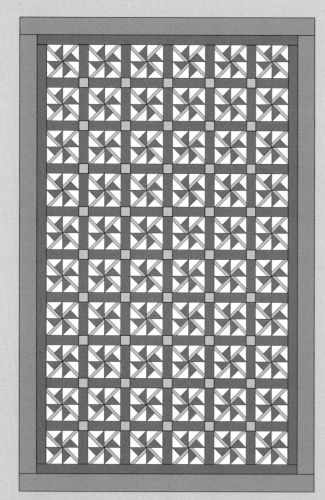

Quilt Layout 1

Or, you could add another 4½" border and only make 45 blocks (set five across and nine down) as in **Quilt Layout 2**.

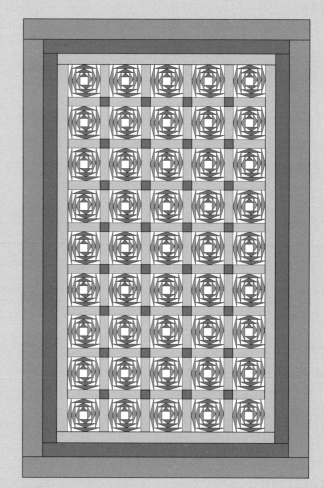

Quilt Layout 2

Some of the blocks, such as the flowers, stars, and log cabin blocks can be placed on point. Add triangles (made by cutting two 5½" squares in half diagonally) to each side and the new block size is 9⅞" finished.

For a twin size quilt, **Quilt Layout 3**, make 45 (five across and nine down) blocks and add a 3" and a 4" border to make a quilt with a finished size of 63³⁄₈" x 102⁷⁄₈".

Or, make 28 blocks (set four across and seven down) with 3" sashing and 4" borders for a quilt, 62¹⁄₂" x 101" as in **Quilt Layout 4**.

Quilt Layout 3

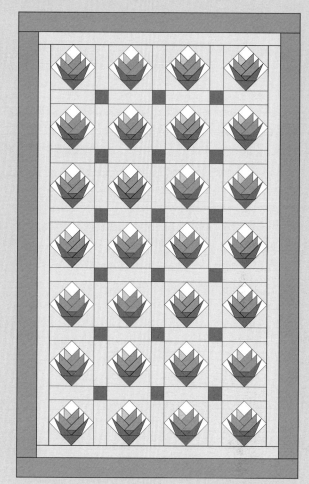

Quilt Layout 4

For quilts in other bed sizes following Quilt Layouts 1 to 4, see chart below.

Layout	Twin	Full	Queen	King

Quilt Layout 1
• 2" sashing &
  3¹⁄₂" border (twin & full)
• 2¹⁄₂" sashing and
  3¹⁄₂" border (queen & king)
	63" x 99"
	6 x 10
	60 blocks
		81" x 99"
		8 x 10
		80 blocks
			85¹⁄₂" x 104¹⁄₂"
			8 x 10
			80 blocks
				104¹⁄₂" x 104¹⁄₂"
				10 x 10
				100 blocks

Quilt Layout 2
• 2" sashing, 3¹⁄₂" &
  4¹⁄₂" borders (twin & full)
• 2¹⁄₂" sashing, 3¹⁄₂" and
  4¹⁄₂" borders (queen & king)
	63" x 99"
	5 x 9
	45 blocks
		81" x 99"
		7 x 9
		63 blocks
			85" x 104"
			7 x 9
			63 blocks
				104" x 104"
				9 x 9
				81 blocks

Quilt Layout 3 • 3" and 4" borders	63³⁄₈" x 102⁷⁄₈" 5 x 9 45 blocks	83¹⁄₈" x 102⁷⁄₈" 7 x 9 63 blocks	83¹⁄₈" x 102⁷⁄₈" 7 x 9 63 blocks	102⁷⁄₈" x 102⁷⁄₈" 9 x 9 81 blocks
Quilt Layout 4 • 3" sashing and 4" border	62¹⁄₂" x 102⁷⁄₈" 4 x 7 28 blocks	75³⁄₈" x 102⁷⁄₈" 5 x 7 35 blocks	88¹⁄₄" x 102⁷⁄₈" 6 x 7 42 blocks	102⁷⁄₈" x 102⁷⁄₈" 7 x 7 49 blocks

Making the Quilt Top

Sew blocks and sashing in rows; sew rows of blocks and sashing together.

Measure quilt top lengthwise; cut two border strips to that size and sew to sides of quilt. Measure quilt top crosswise, including borders just added and cut two border strips to that size. Sew to top and bottom of quilt top. Repeat for any remaining borders.

Remove paper or Tear Away® backing at this time. **Hint:** *Use a spray bottle of water to dampen paper for easier removal.*

Marking the Quilting Design

Before marking on your quilt top, be sure to test any marking material to make sure it will wash out of your fabric. Mark all quilting lines on the right side of the fabric. For marking, use a hard lead pencil, chalk or other special quilt marking materials. If you quilt right on the marked lines, they will not show.

A word of caution: Marking lines which are intended to disappear after quilting - either by exposure to air or with water - may become permanent when set with a hot iron. Therefore, don't iron your quilt top after you have marked your quilting pattern.

If you are quilting around shapes, you may not need to mark your line if you feel that you can accurately gauge the quilting line as you work. If you are quilting "in the ditch" of the seam (the space right in the seam), marking is not necessary. Other quilting will need to be marked.

If you plan to tie your quilt, you do not need to mark it.

Attaching the Batting and Backing

There are a number of different types of batting on the market. Choose the one that is right for your quilt. Very thin cotton batting will require a great deal of quilting to hold it (quilting lines no more than 1" apart); very thick batting should be used only for tied quilts. A medium-loft bonded polyester batting is a good choice for machine quilting.

Hint: Remove batting from its packaging a day in advance and open it out full size. This will help the batting to lie flat.

Use 100% cotton fabric for the backing of your quilt. Bed sheets are usually not good backing materials. If you are making a bed-sized quilt, you will most likely have to piece your fabric to fit the quilt top. Cut off the selvages and sew pieces together carefully; press seams open. This is the only time in making a quilt that seams should be pressed open. Cut batting and backing about 2" larger than the quilt top on all sides. Place backing, wrong side up, on a flat surface. Place batting centered on top of backing, then center quilt right side up on batting.

The layers of the quilt must now be held together before quilting. There are three methods: thread basting, safety pin basting and quilt gun basting.

For **thread basting**, baste with long stitches, starting in the center and sewing toward the edges in a number of diagonal lines.

For **safety pin basting**, pin through all layers at once starting from the center and working out to the edges. Place the pins no more than 4" to 6" apart. Think of your quilt plan as you work and make certain that your pins avoid the prospective quilting lines. Choose rustproof pins that are #1 or #2. To make pinning easier, many quilters use a quilter's spoon. The spoon is notched so that it can push the point of the safety pin closed.

For **quilt gun basting**, use the handy trigger tool (found in quilt and fabric stores) that pushes nylon tags through all layers of the quilt. Start in the center and work randomly toward the outside edges. Place tags about 4" apart. You can sew right over the tags and then they can be easily removed by cutting off with a pair of scissors.

Quilting

Your quilt can be either machine or hand quilted. **Note:** *Hand quilting may be a little more difficult if fabric or muslin was used as a foundation since there is an extra layer of fabric to quilt through.* If you have never used a sewing machine for quilting, you might want to read more about the technique. Quilting for People Who Don't Have Time to Quilt, Book #4111 by Marti Michell and A Beginner's Guide to Machine Quilting, Book # 4121 by Judi Tyrrell, both published by ASN Publishing, are excellent introductions to machine quilting. These books are available at your local quilt store or department, or write the publisher for a list of sources.

You do not need a special machine for quilting. You can machine quilt with almost any home sewing machine. Just make sure that it is oiled and in good working condition. An even-feed foot is a good investment if you are going to machine quilt since it is designed to feed the top and bottom layers of the quilt through the machine evenly.

Use fine transparent nylon thread in the top and regular sewing thread in the bobbin.

To **quilt in the ditch** of a seam (this is actually stitching in the space between two pieces of fabric that have been sewn together), use your fingers to pull the blocks or pieces apart and machine stitch right between the two pieces. Try to keep your stitching just to the side of the seam that does not have the bulk of the seam allowance under it. When you have finished stitching, the quilting will be practically hidden in the seam.

Free form machine quilting is done with a darning foot and the feed dogs down on your sewing machine. It can be used to quilt around a design or to quilt a motif. Mark your quilting design as described in Marking the Quilting Design on page 10. Free form machine quilting takes practice to master because you are controlling the quilt through the machine rather than the machine moving the quilt. With free form machine quilting, you can quilt in any direction—up and down, side to side and even in circles without pivoting the quilt around the needle.

Attaching the Binding

Place the quilt on a flat surface and carefully trim the backing and batting $1/2$" beyond the quilt top edge. Measure the quilt top and cut two $2^1/2$"-wide binding strips the length of your quilt (for sides). Fold strips in half lengthwise wrong sides together. Place one strip along one side of the quilt; sew with a $1/4$" seam allowance, **Fig 16** (seam allowance should be measured from outer edge of quilt top fabric, not outer edge of batting/backing).

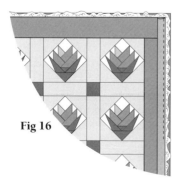

Fig 16

Turn binding to back and slipstitch to backing covering previous stitching line, **Fig 17**. Repeat on other side.

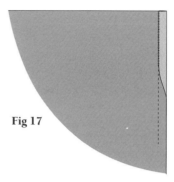

Fig 17

For top and bottom edges, measure quilt crosswise and cut two $2^1/2$"-wide strips that size adding $1/2$" to each end. Fold strips in half lengthwise with wrong sides together. Place one strip along top edge with $1/2$" extending beyond each side; sew with a $1/4$" seam allowance, **Fig 18**. Turn binding to back and tuck the extra $1/2$" under at each end; slipstitch to backing fabric.

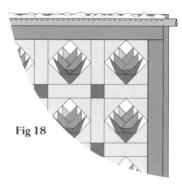

Fig 18

The Finishing Touch

When your quilt is finished, always sign and date it. A label can be cross stitched, embroidered or even written with a permanent marking pen. Hand stitch to back of quilt.

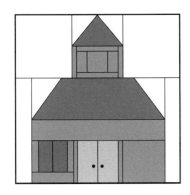

School House

Photographed block note: *Two black pony beads were sewn on doors.*

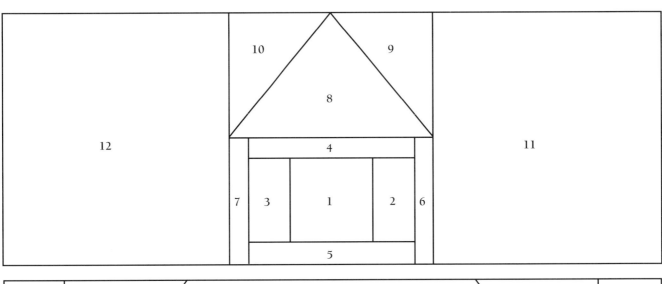

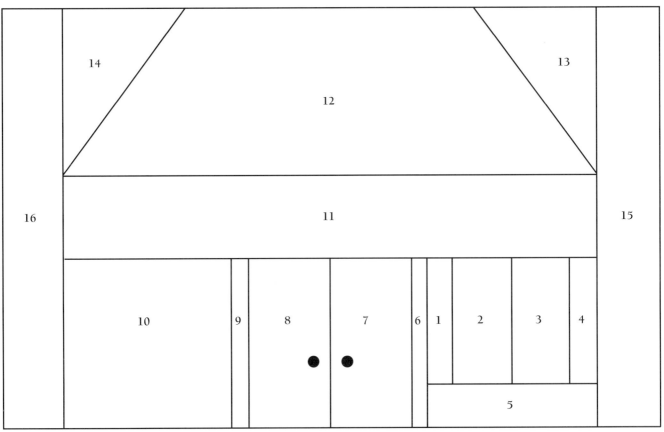

2  Butterfly Charmer

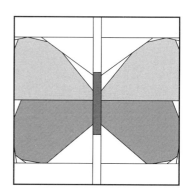

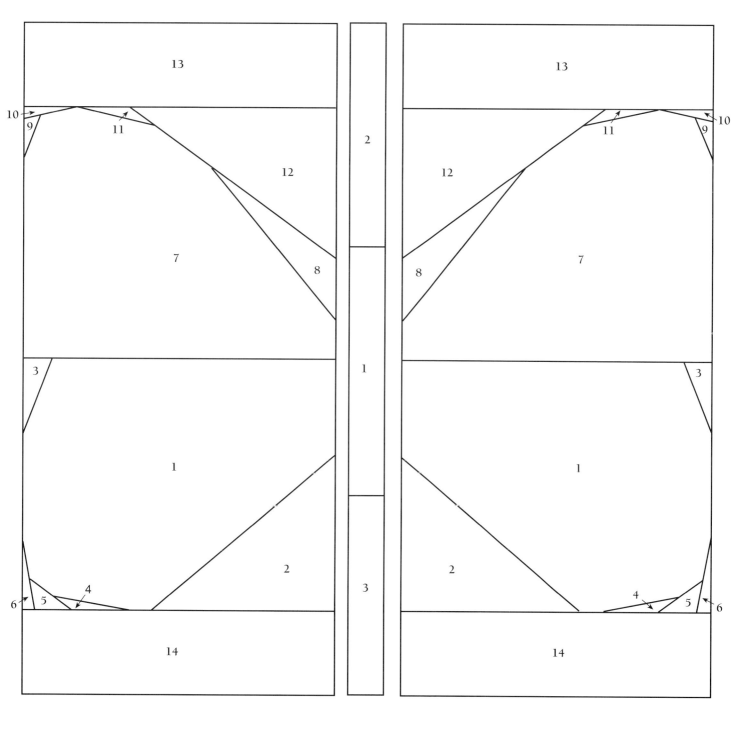

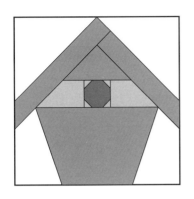

Birdhouse

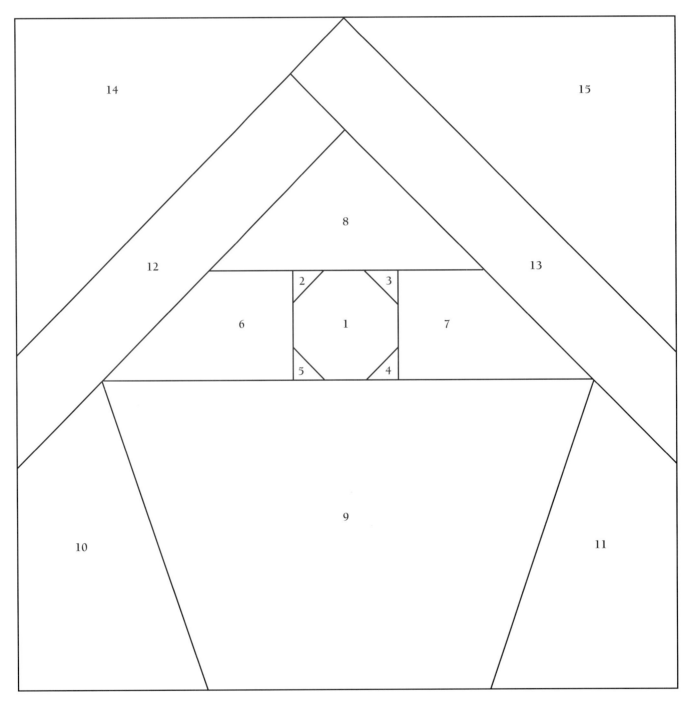

4 Bird in Flight

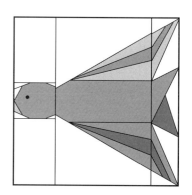

Photographed block note: One black pony bead was sewn on bird's head for eye.

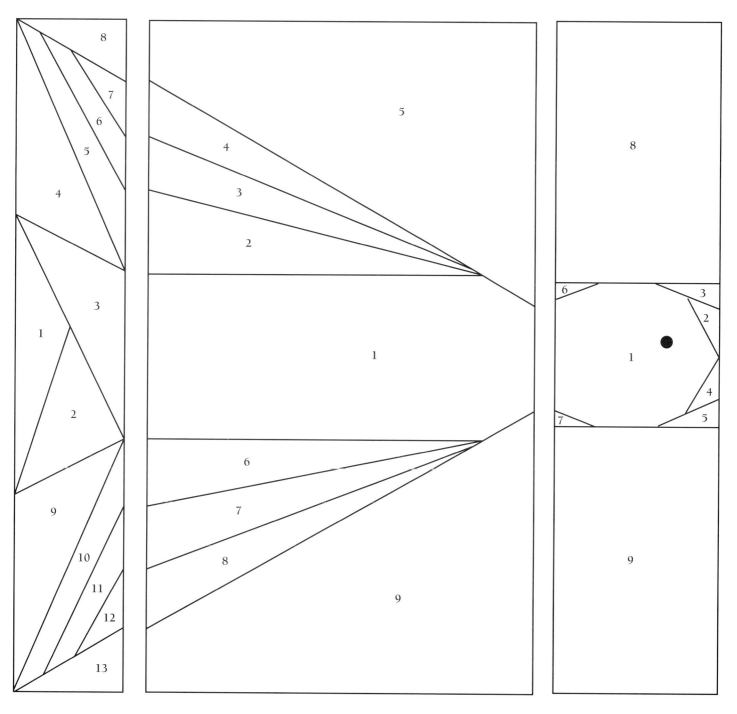

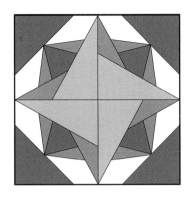

Twisting Star

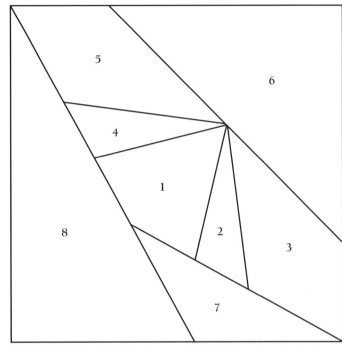

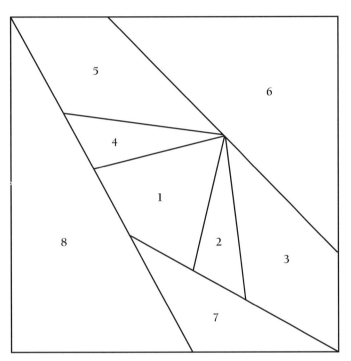

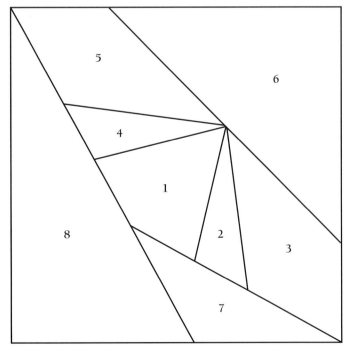

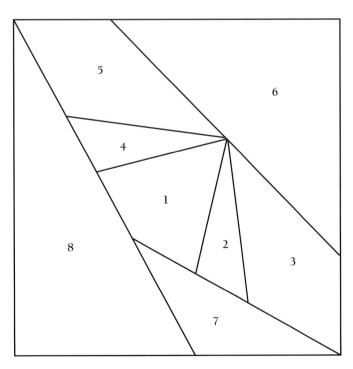

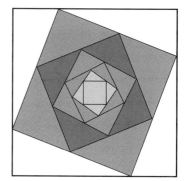

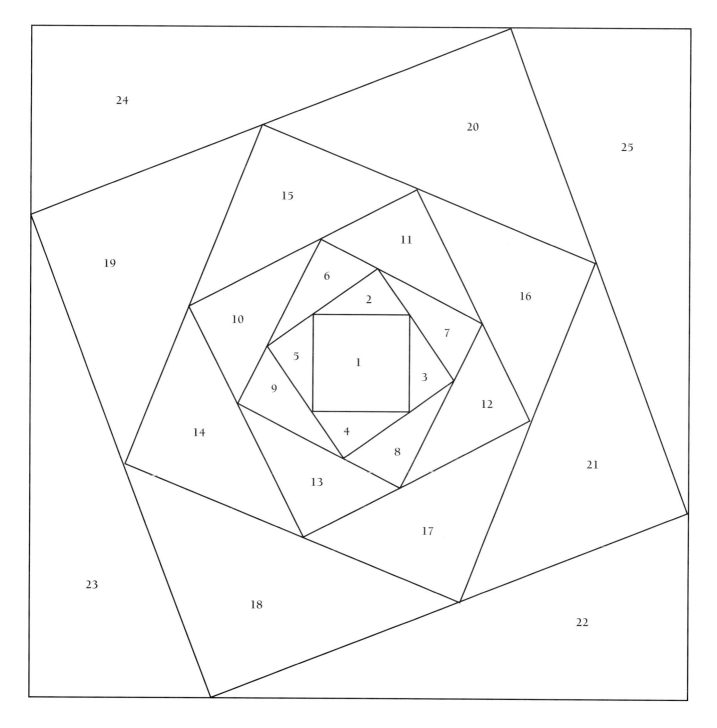

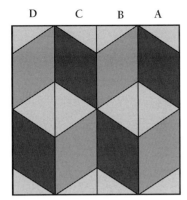

D C B A

7 Tumbling Blocks

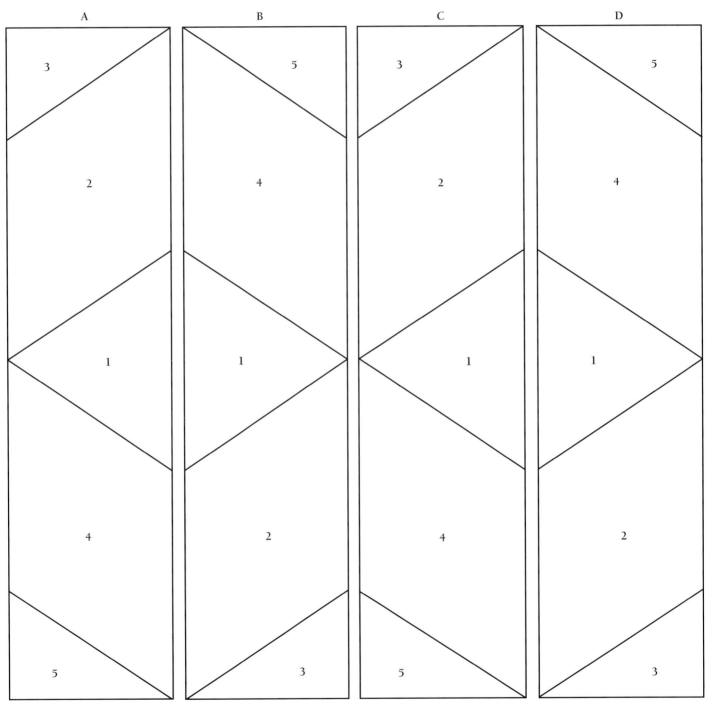

A

3
2
1
4
5

B

5
4
1
2
3

C

3
2
1
4
5

D

5
4
1
2
3

Teddy Bear

Photographed block notes: *Two $1/2$"-diameter black buttons were used for eyes; one $3/4$"-diameter tan button was used for nose; and mouth was embroidered with three strands of brown floss.*

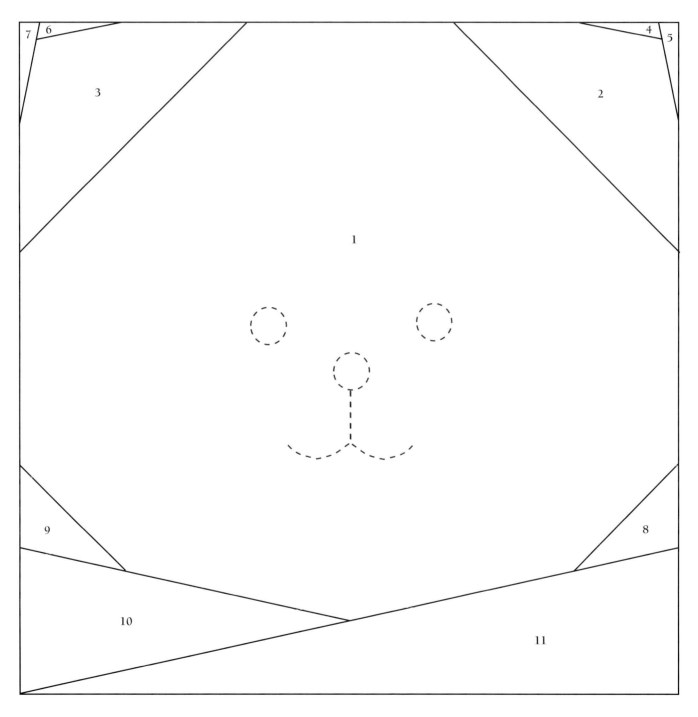

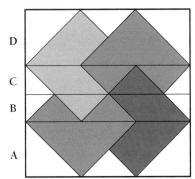

9 Card Tricks

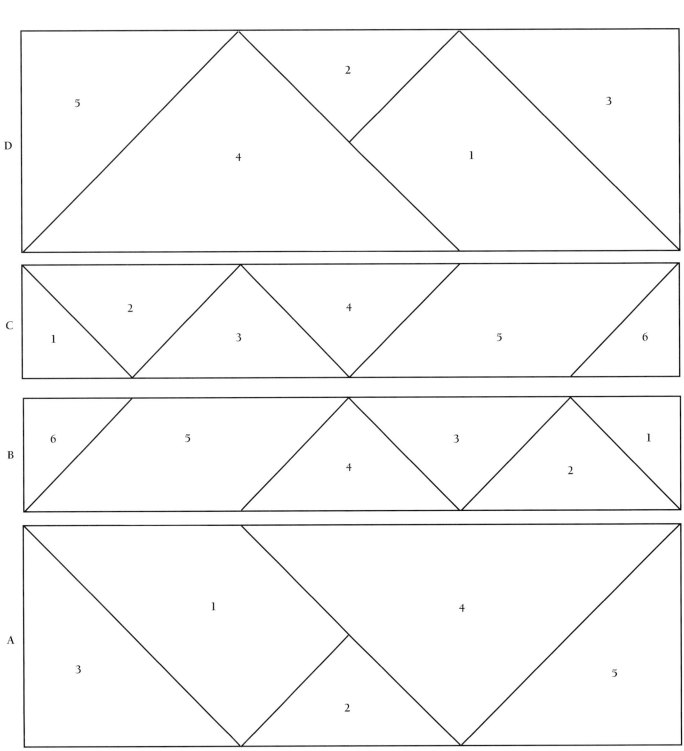

 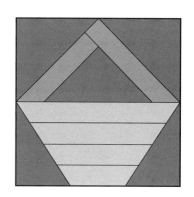

Basket

Photographed block notes: *Two butterfly buttons ($^5/_8$" and $^7/_8$"-wide) and seven assorted buttons ($^1/_2$" to $^3/_4$" diameter) were sewn on the basket.*

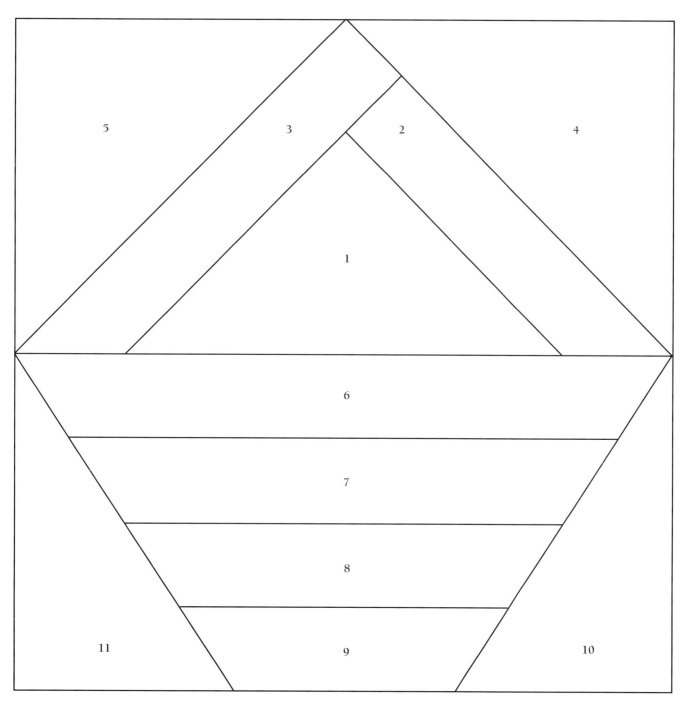

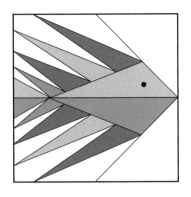

11 Tropical Fish

Photographed block note: *One ³/₈"-diameter black button was sewn on fish for eye.*

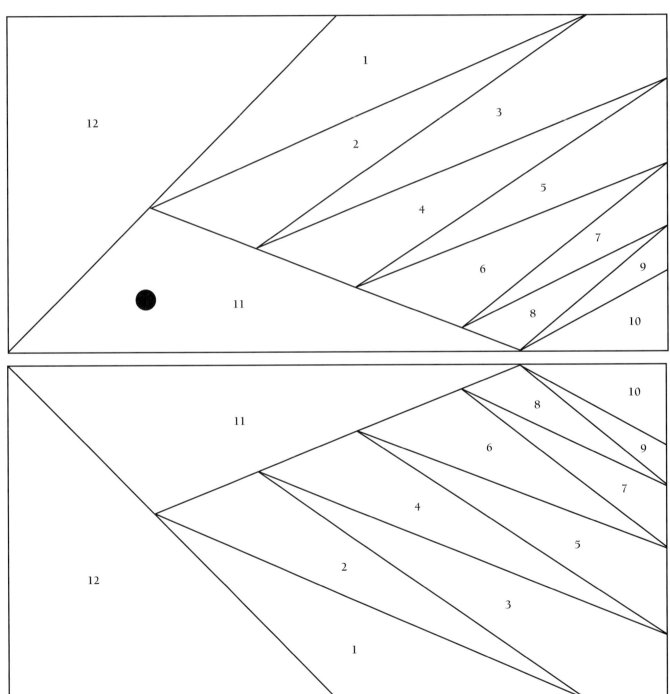

 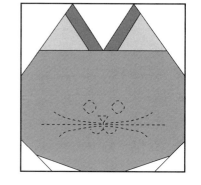

Cheerful Cat

Photographed block note: *Two ¹/₂″-square green buttons were sewn on cat for eyes; the nose was hand embroidered with three strands of pink floss; and the mouth and whiskers were hand embroidered with three strands of gray floss.*

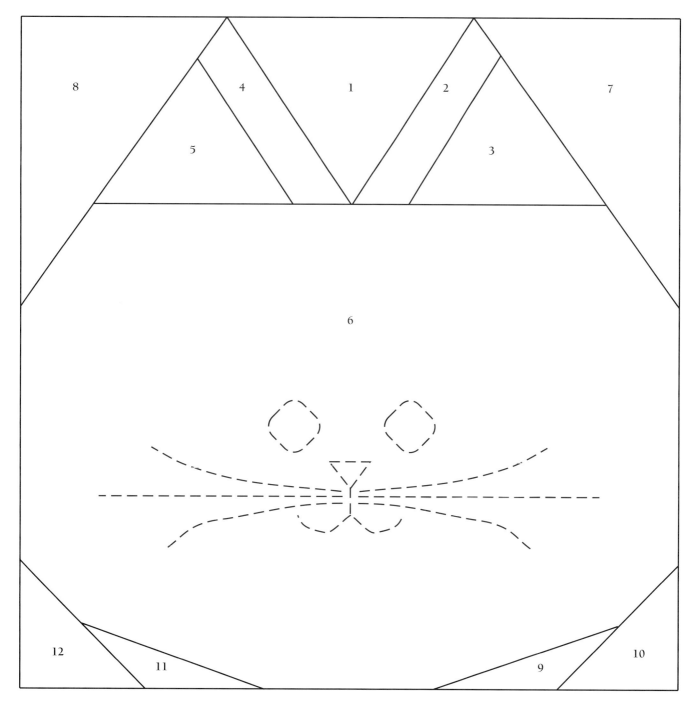

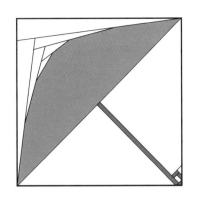

13  Umbrella

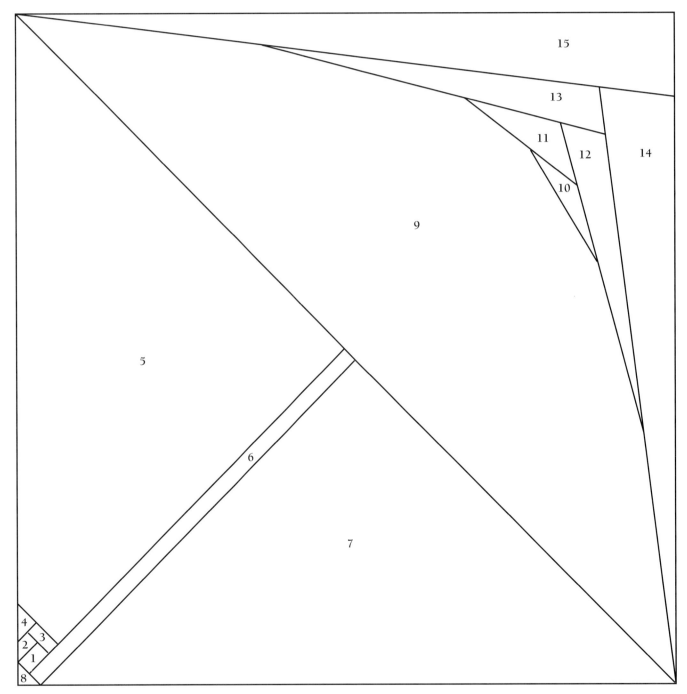

14 Pineapple Log Cabin

15 Log Cabin Triangles

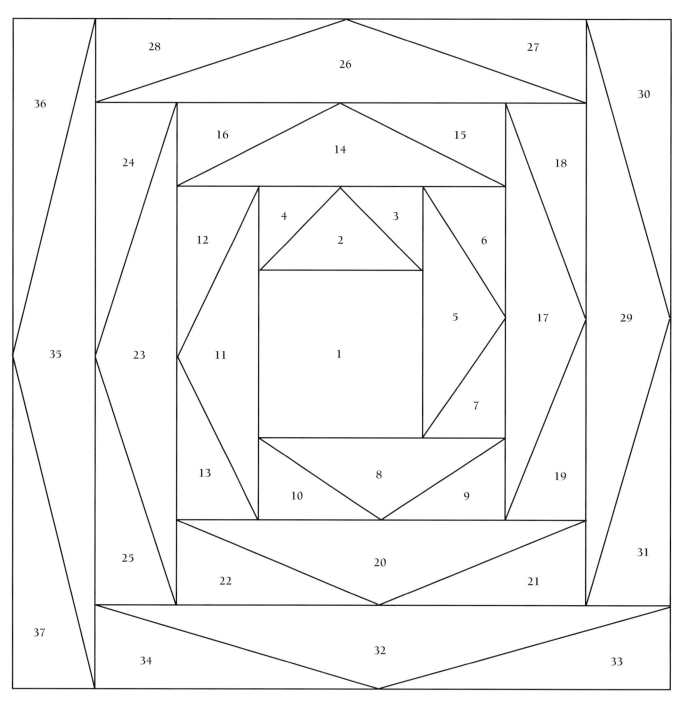

16 Potted Plant

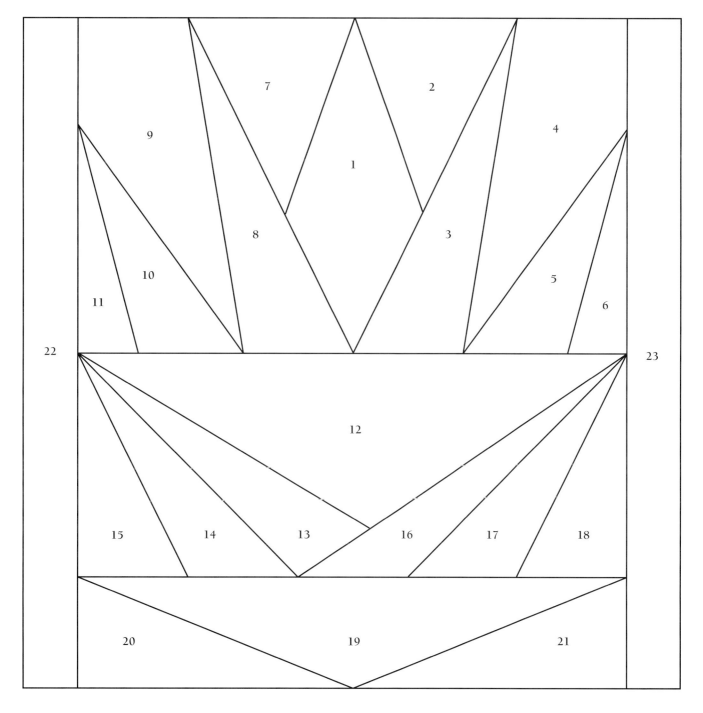

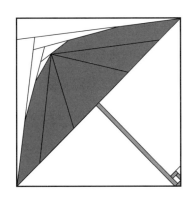

17

Parasol

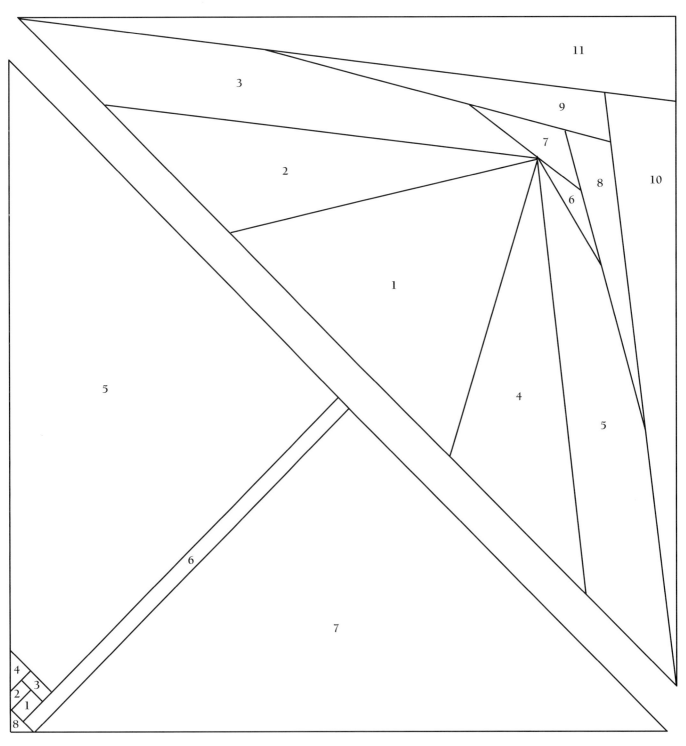

Boy

Photographed block note: *Two black seed beads were sewn on face for eyes.*

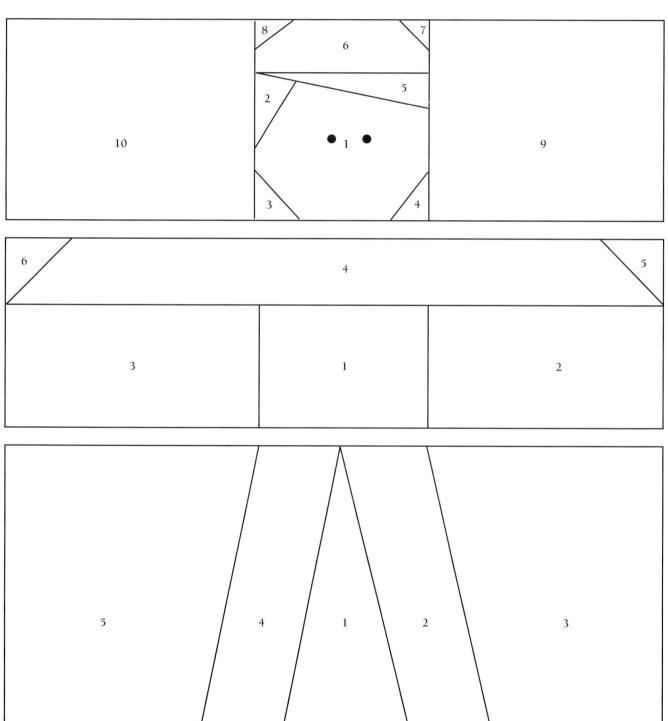

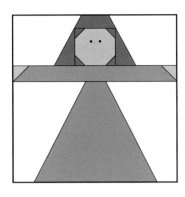

Photographed block note: *Two blue seed beads were sewn on face for eyes.*

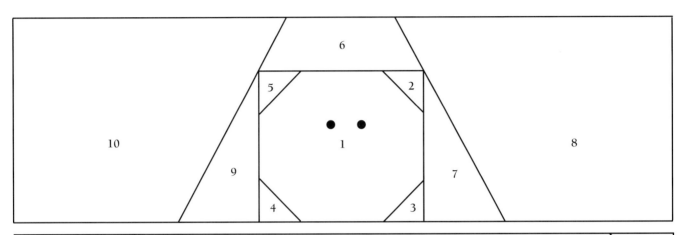

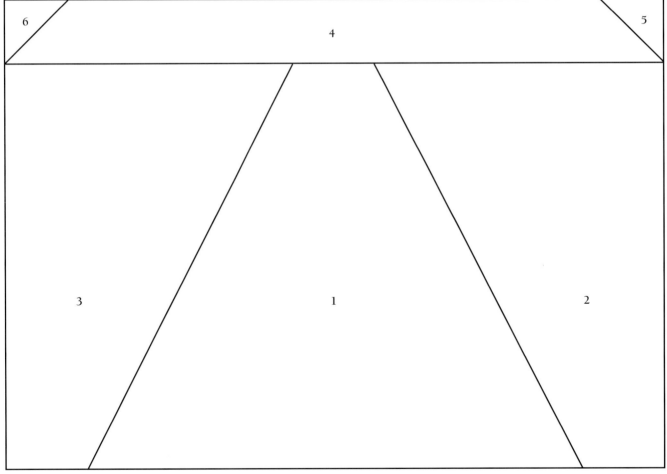

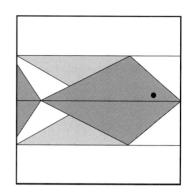

Fish

Photographed block note: *One ³/₈"-diameter blue button was sewn on fish for eye.*

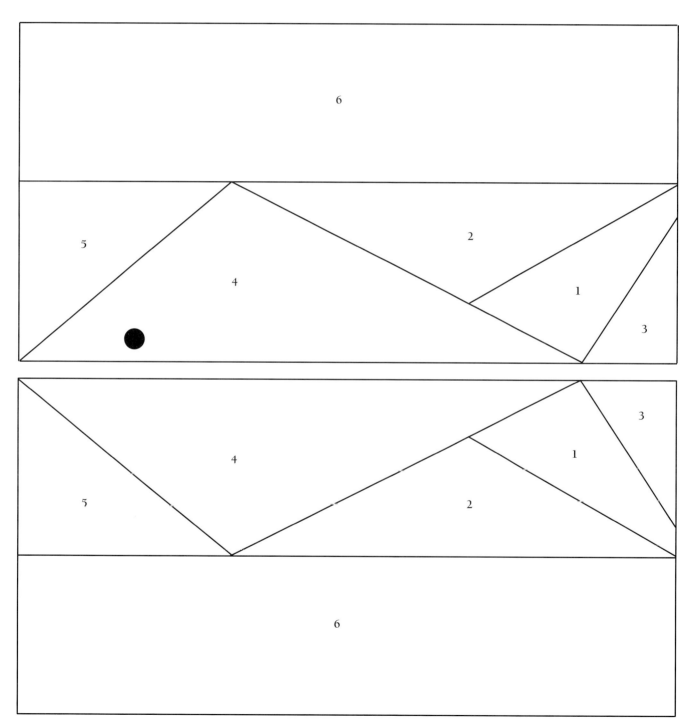

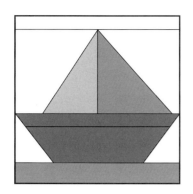

Sailboat

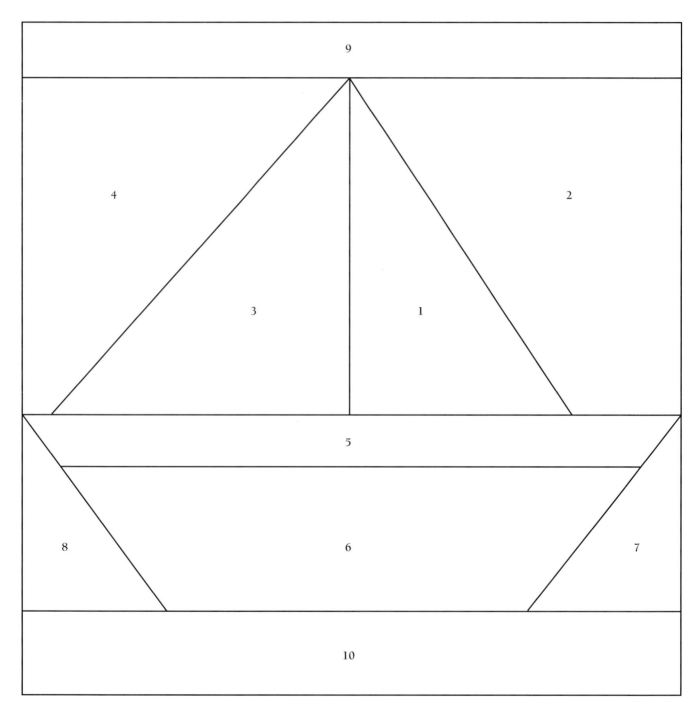

Airplane

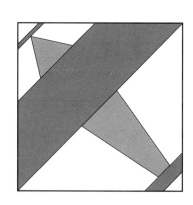

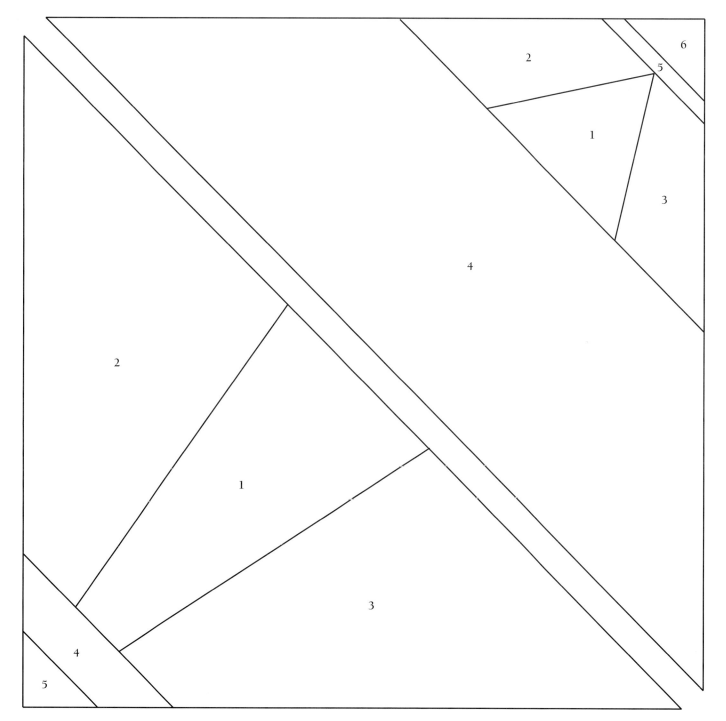

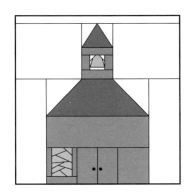

Church

Photographed block note: *Two black pony beads were sewn on doors.*

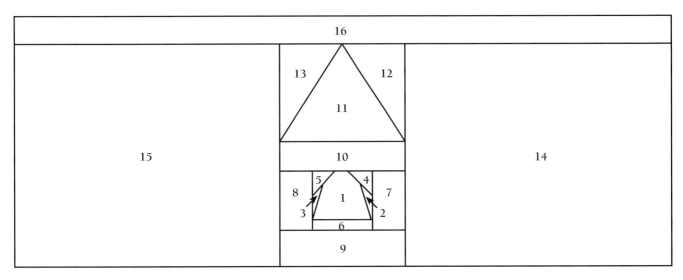

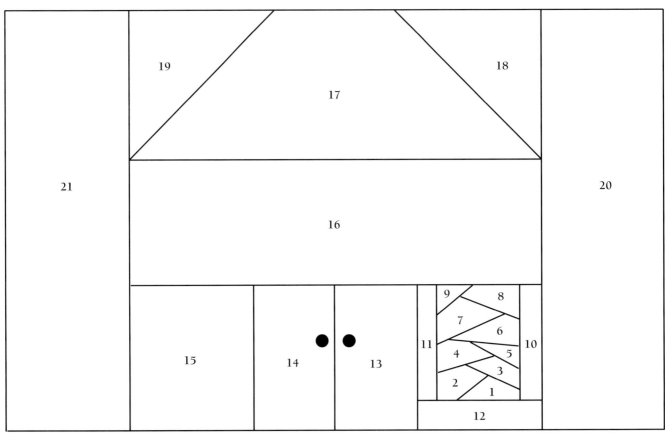

 **24**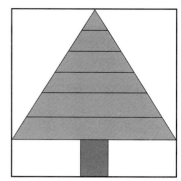

Tree of Strips

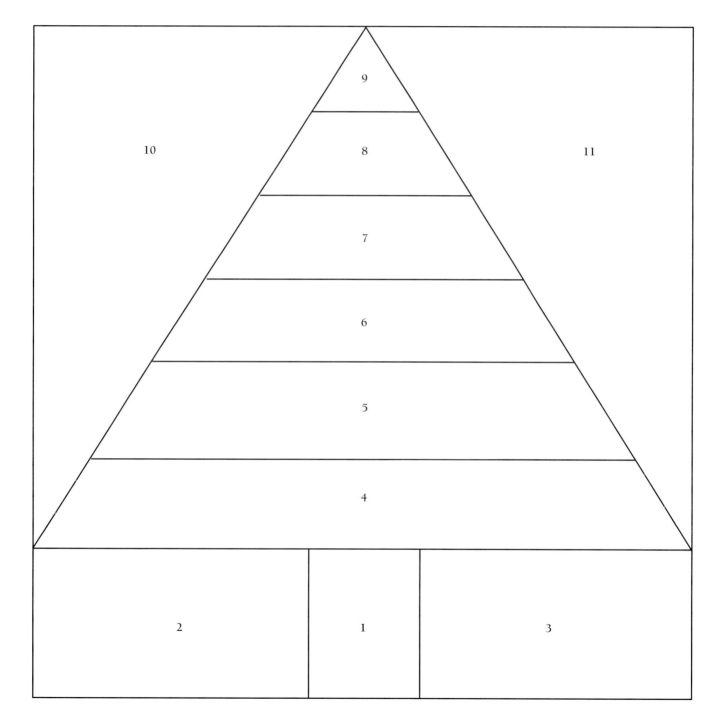

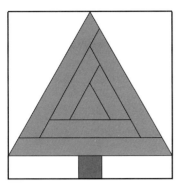

Log Cabin Tree

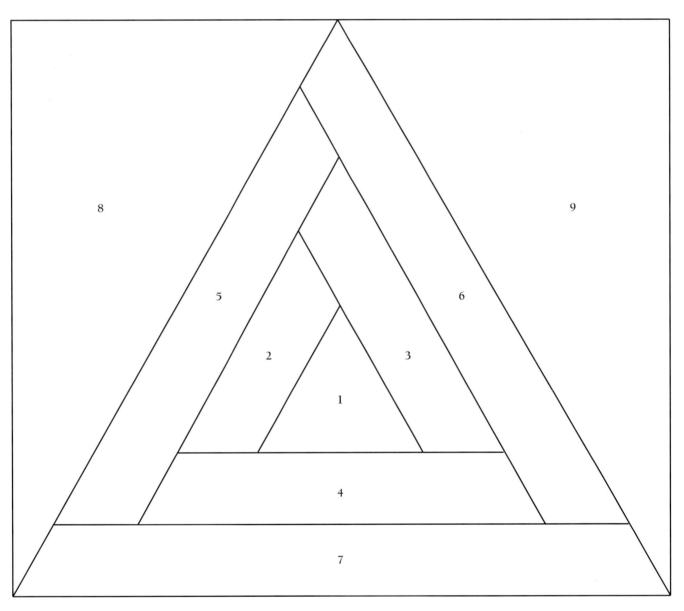

 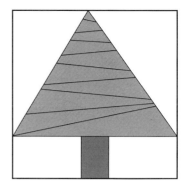

Crazy Tree

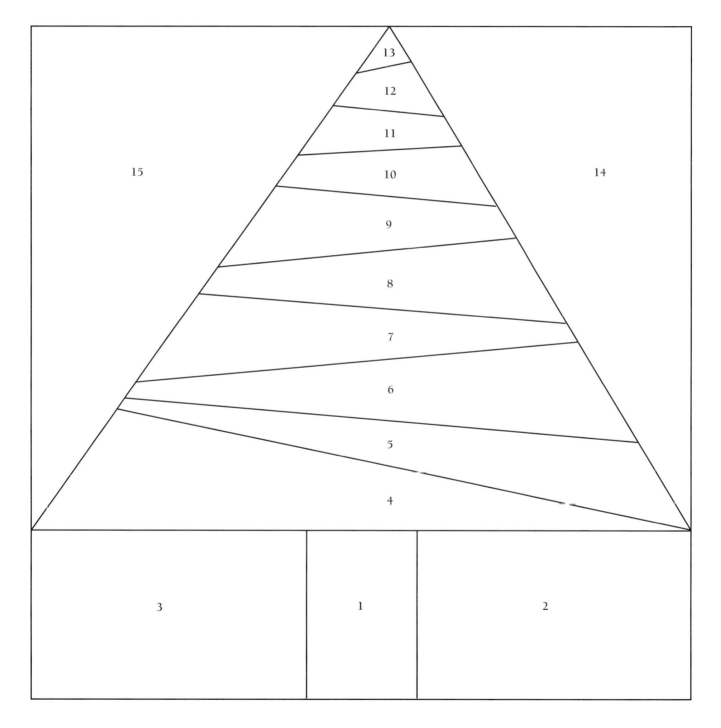

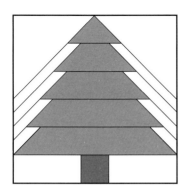

27 Christmas Tree

18 16 17

15 13 14

12 10 11

9 7 8

6 4 5

3 1 2

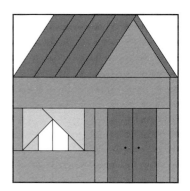

Photographed block note: *Two black pony beads were sewn on doors.*

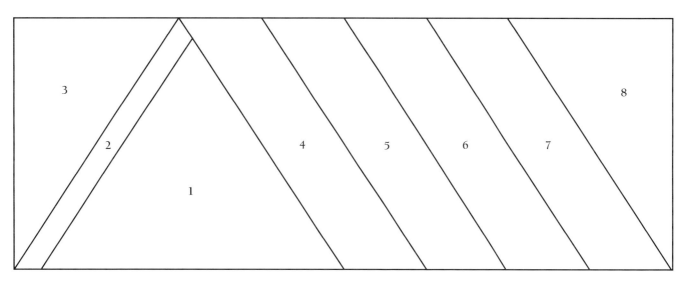

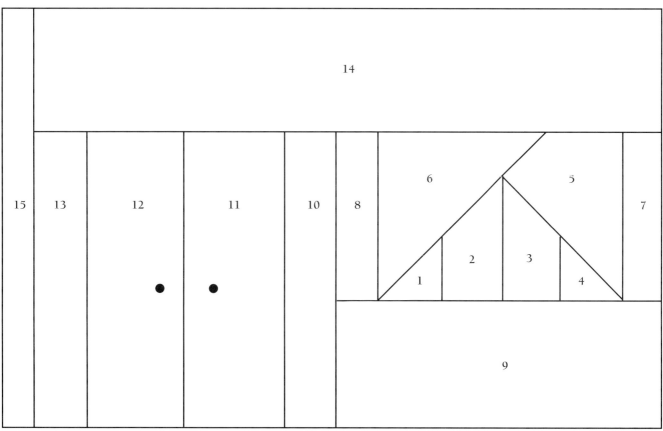

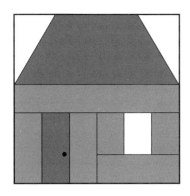

Bungalow

Photographed block note: *One blue pony bead was sewn on door.*

11	10
	9	

8

3	1	2	5	6	7

4

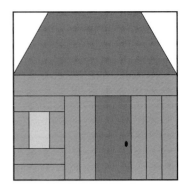

Manor House

Photographed block note: *One black 3mm bead was sewn on door.*

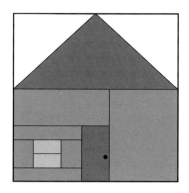

Country House

Photographed block note: *One 6mm gold bead was sewn on door.*

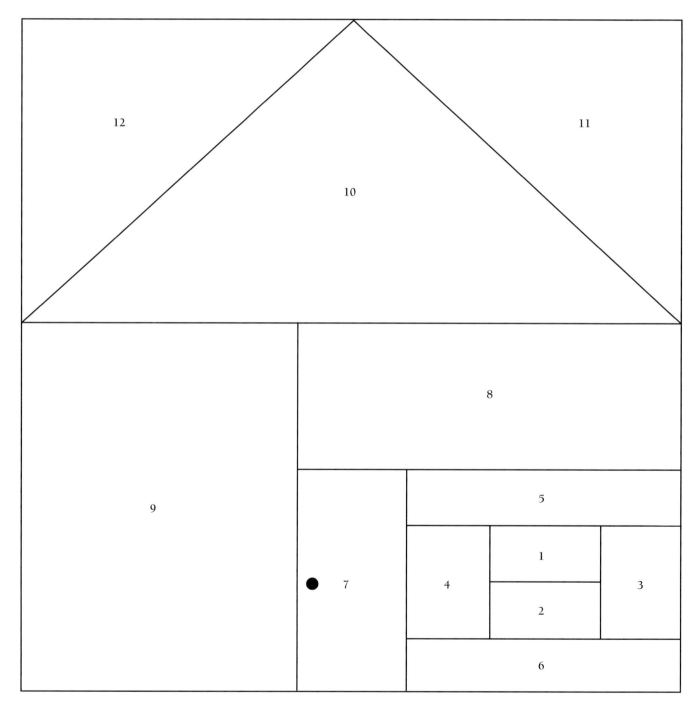

32 Sunbonnet Sue

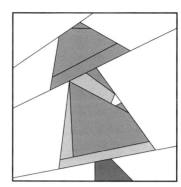

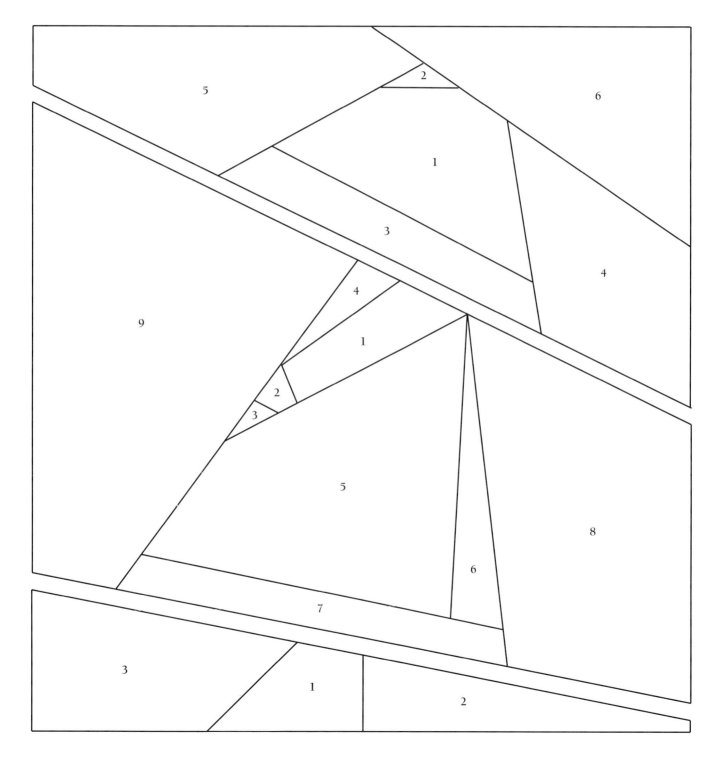

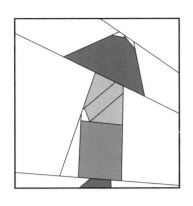

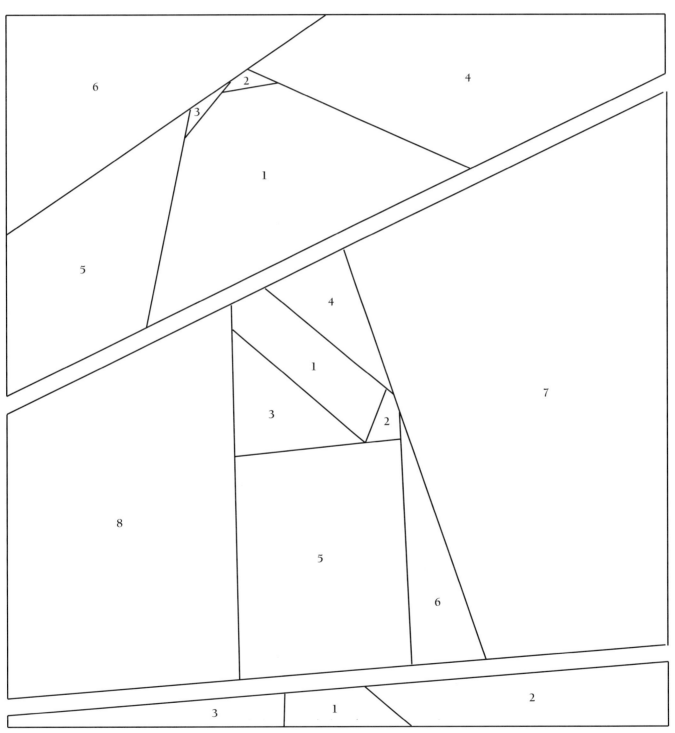

34 Square in a Square

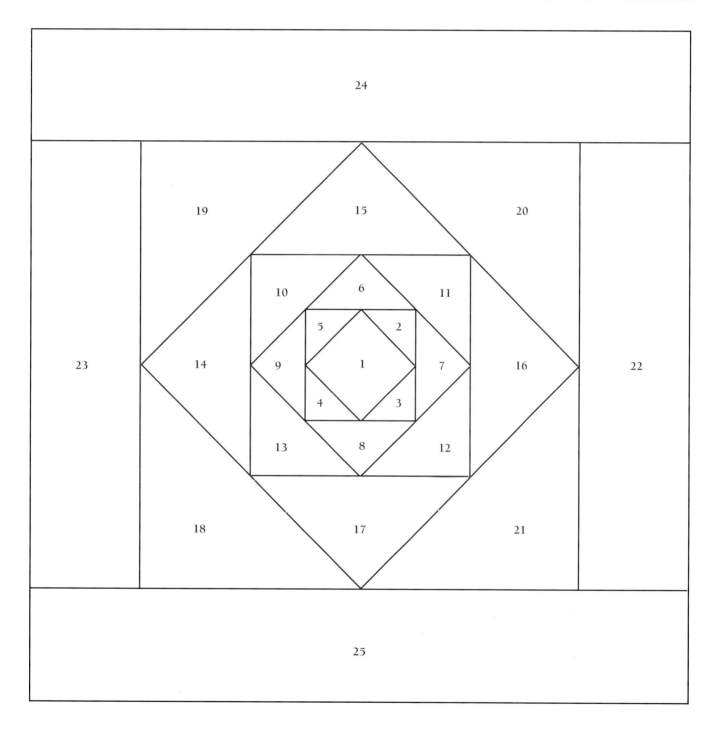

35 Shadow Geese

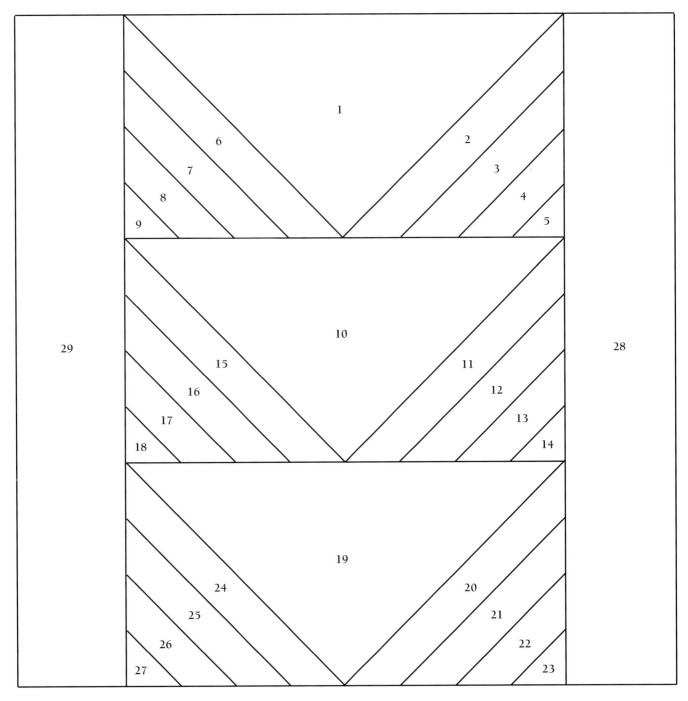

36 Diamond Log Cabin

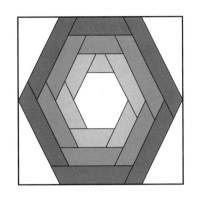

37 Hexagon Log Cabin

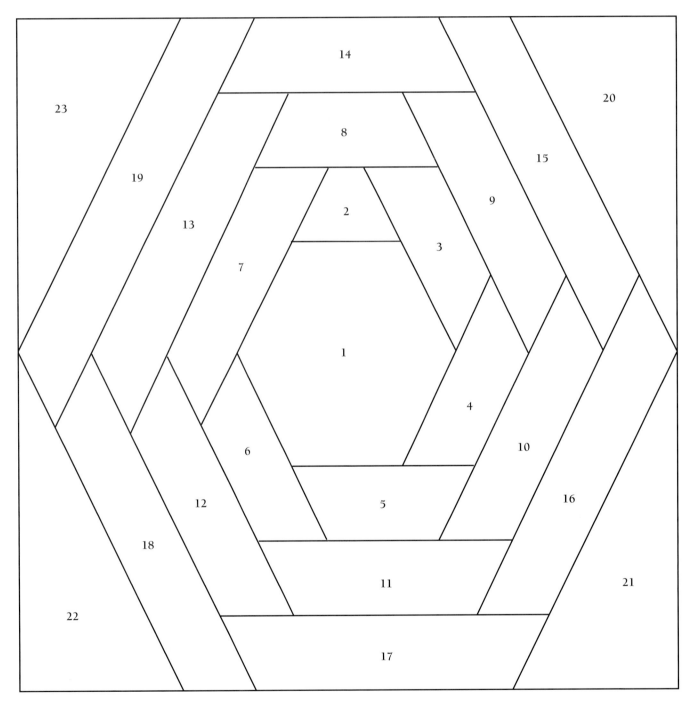

49

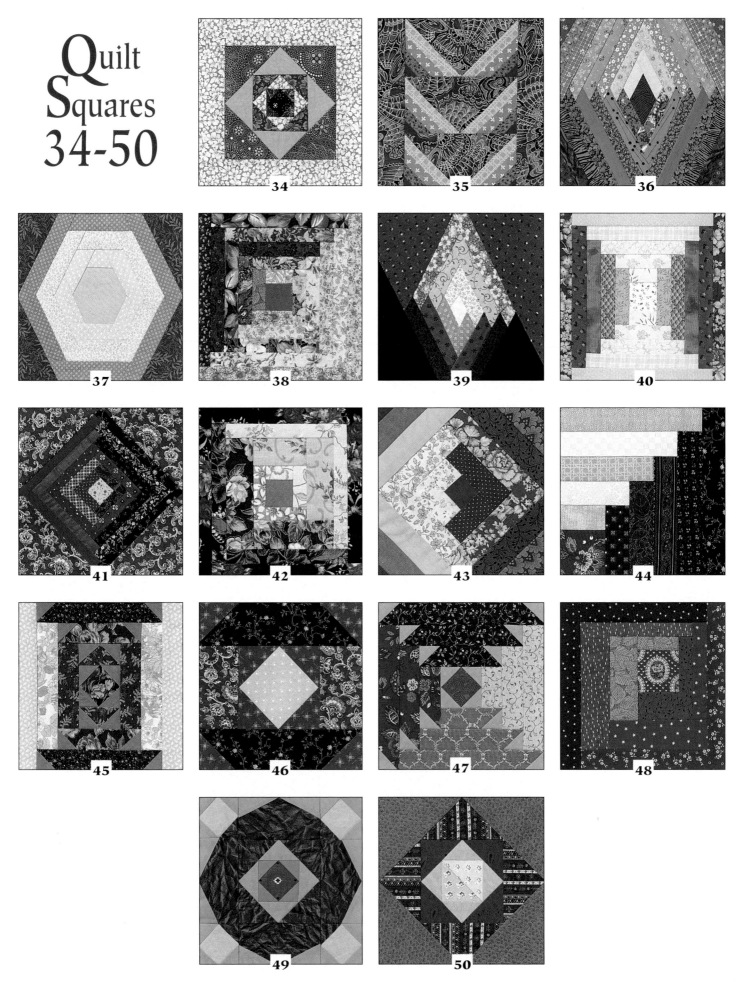

Quilt Squares 34-50

34

35

36

37

38

39

40

41

42

43

44

45

46

47

48

49

50

Quilt
Squares
51-67

51

Quilt Squares 68-84

68

69

70

71

72

73

74

75

76

77

78

79

80

81

82

83

84

38 Traditional Log Cabin

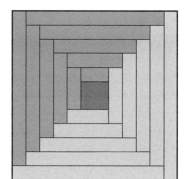

						18					
						14					
						10					
						6					
						2					
21	17	13	9	5		1	3	7	11	15	19
						4					
						8					
						12					
						16					
						20					

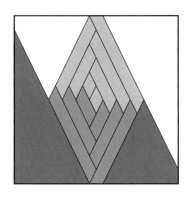

39 Log Cabin Diamond

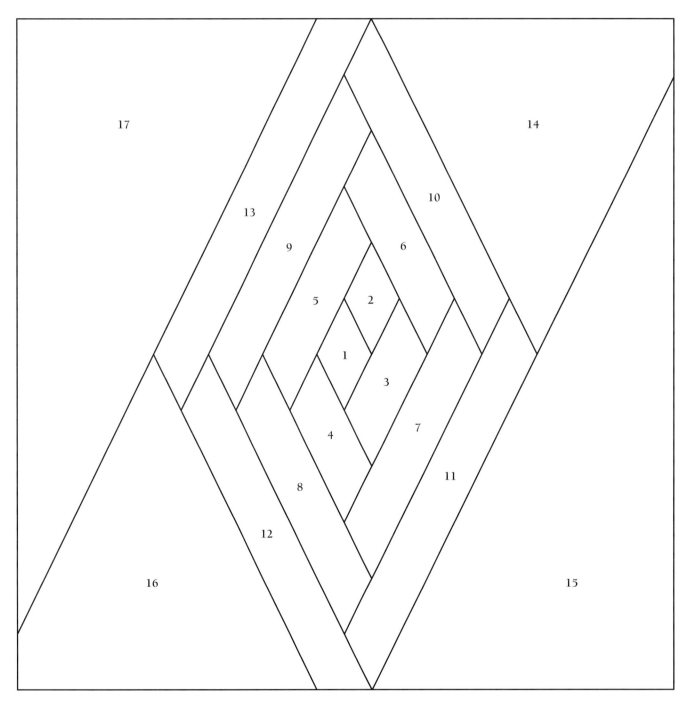

40 Courthouse Steps

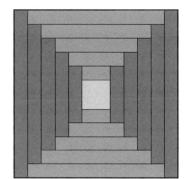

						18						
						14						
						10						
						6						
						2						
21	17	13	9	5		1		4	8	12	16	20
						3						
						7						
						11						
						15						
						19						

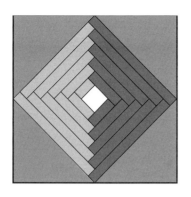

Log Cabin on Point

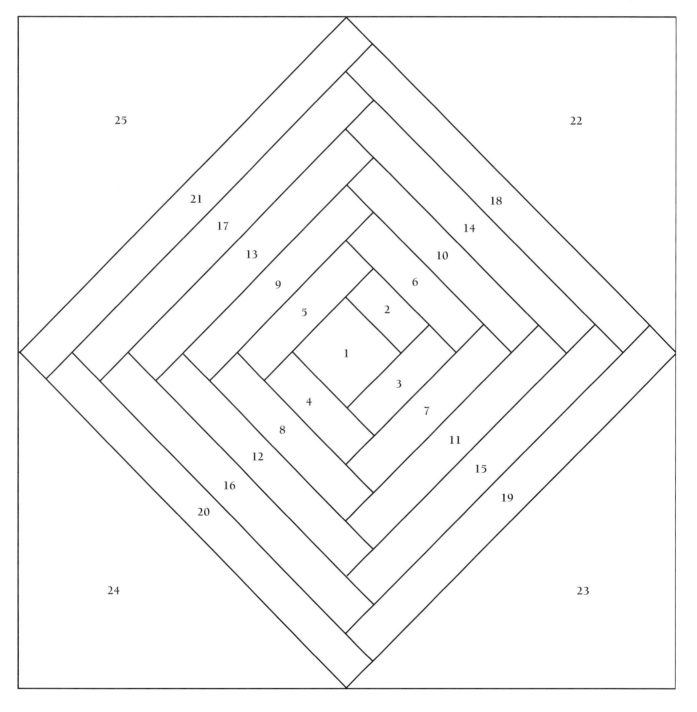

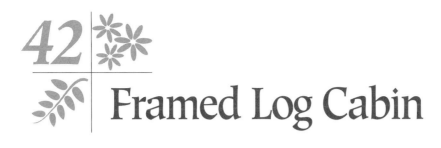

42 Framed Log Cabin

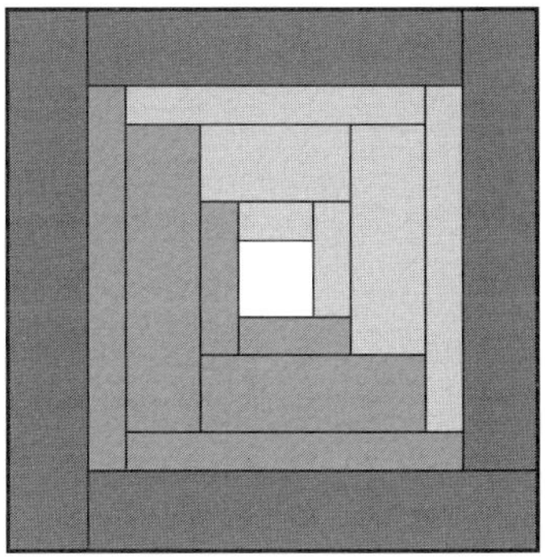

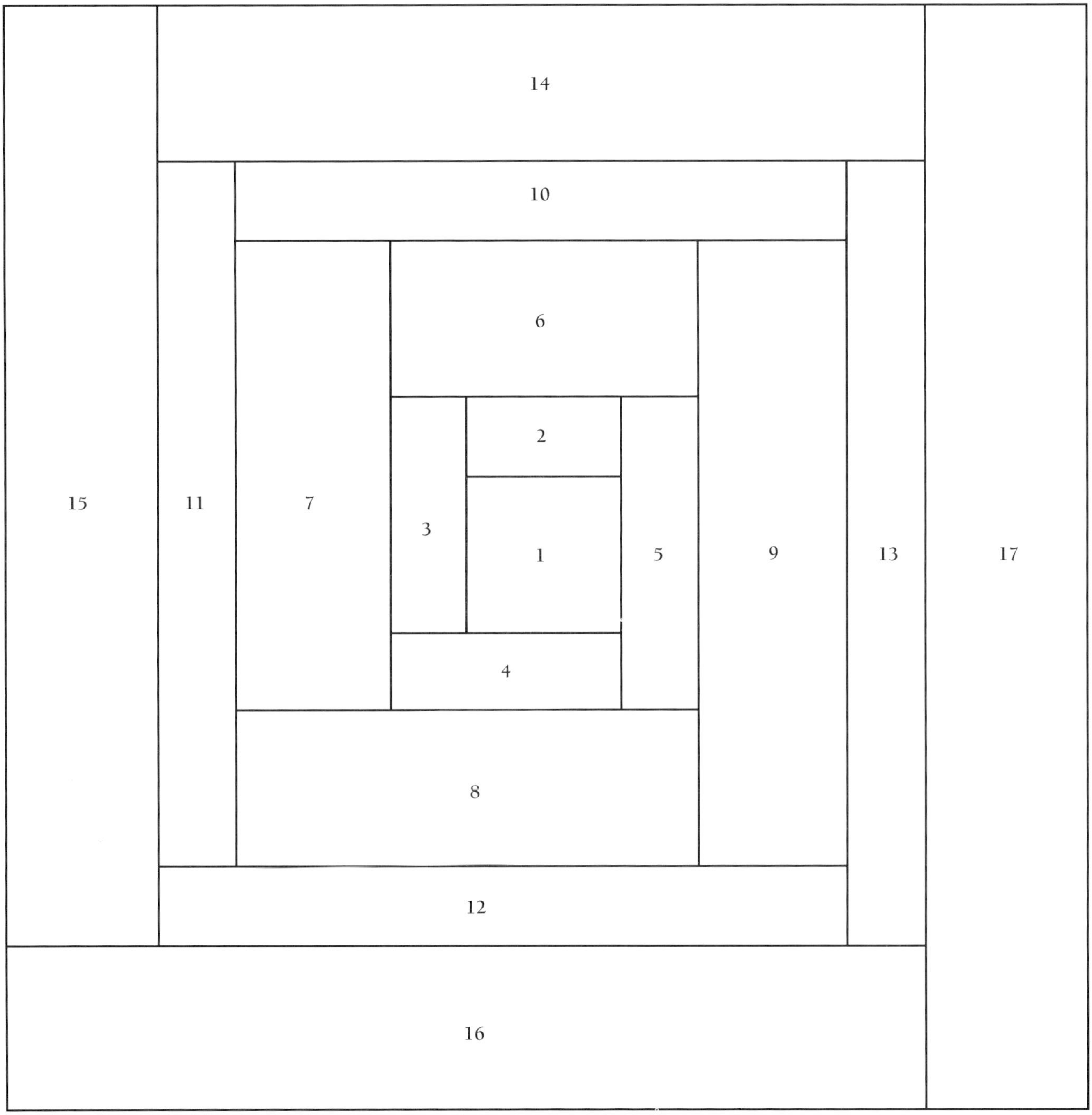
14
10
6
2
15
11
7
3
1
5
9
13
17
4
8
12
16

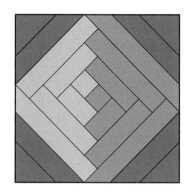

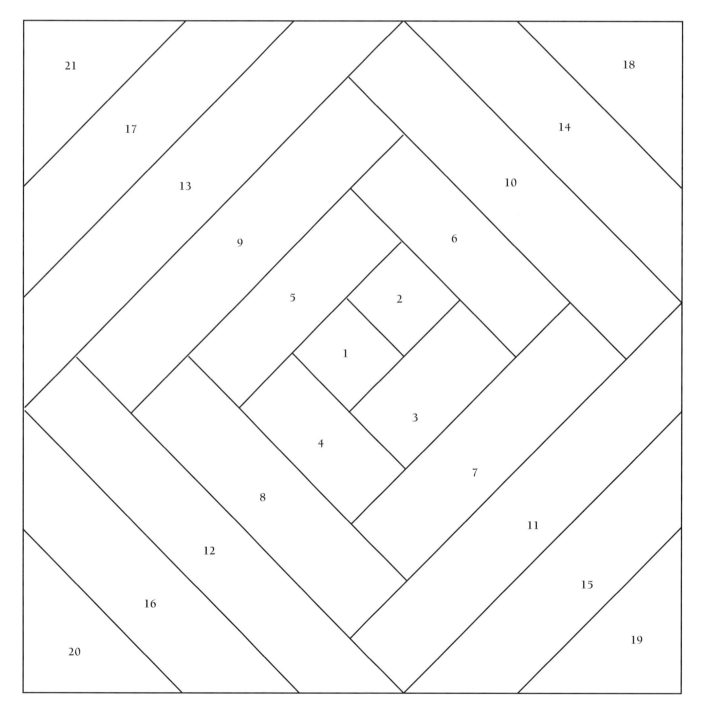

44 Off-Center Log Cabin

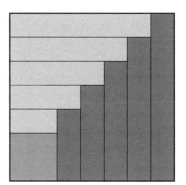

```
┌─────┬──────────────────────────────────────────────┐
│     │                                              │
│     │                     10                       │
│     ├─────────┬────────────────────────────────────┤
│     │         │                                    │
│     │         │                 8                  │
│     │         ├──────────┬─────────────────────────┤
│     │         │          │                         │
│     │         │          │            6            │
│     │         │          ├──────┬──────────────────┤
│  11 │    9    │    7     │      │        4         │
│     │         │          │      ├──────┬───────────┤
│     │         │          │  5   │      │     2     │
│     │         │          │      │  3   ├───────────┤
│     │         │          │      │      │           │
│     │         │          │      │      │     1     │
│     │         │          │      │      │           │
└─────┴─────────┴──────────┴──────┴──────┴───────────┘
```

Log Cabin Variation I

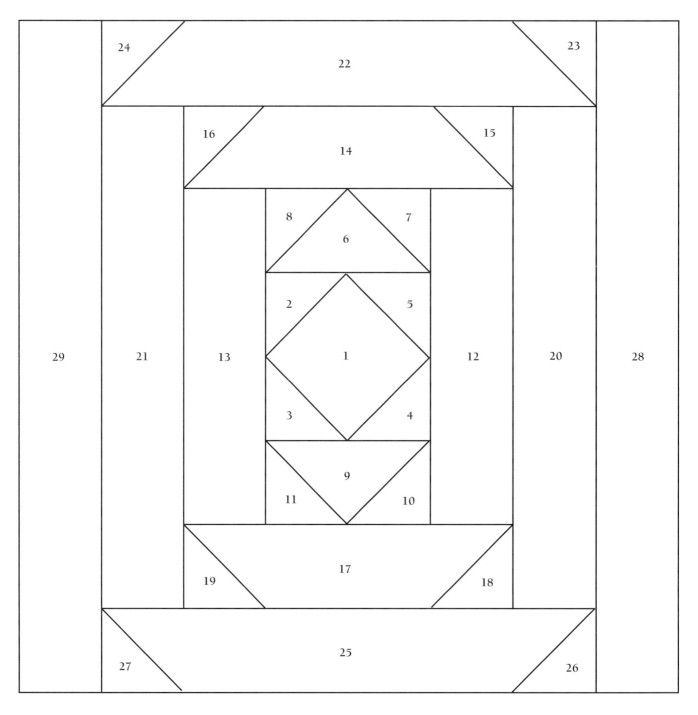

46 Kansas Dugout

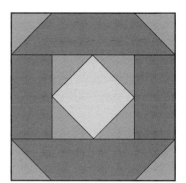

10

9

8

3

2

7

1

6

4

5

11

13

12

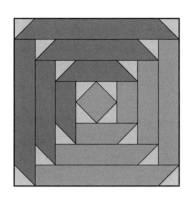

Log Cabin Variation II

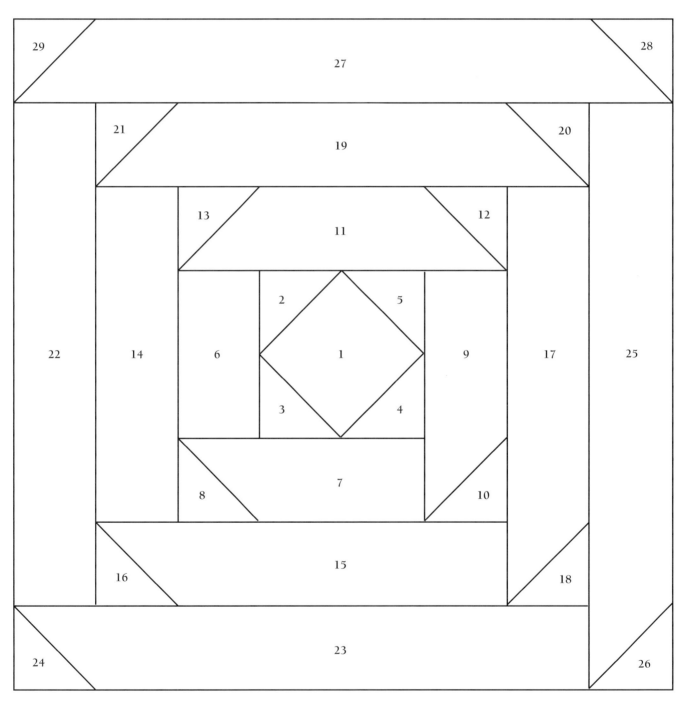

48 Uneven Log Cabin

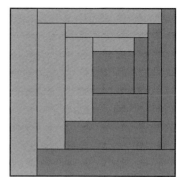

				10				
				6				
			2					
11	7	3		1		5	9	13
			4					
			8					
			12					

49

Storm at Sea

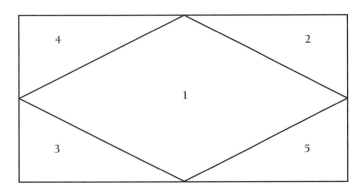

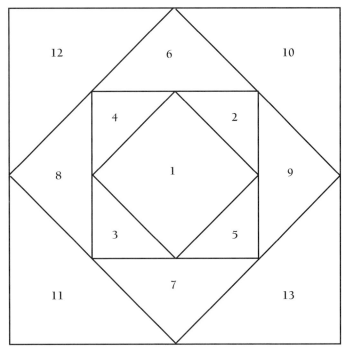

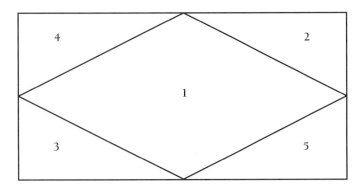

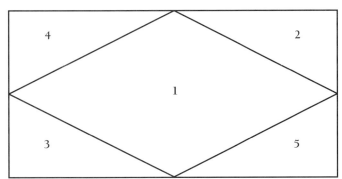

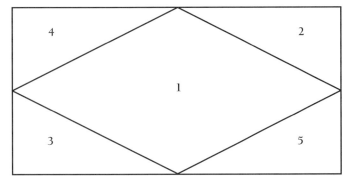

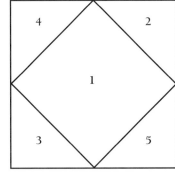

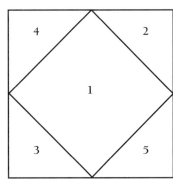

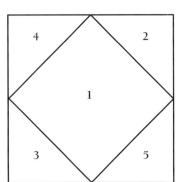

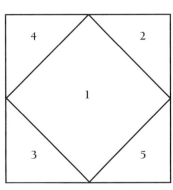

50 Block in a Block

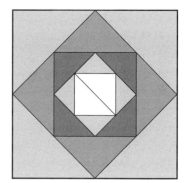

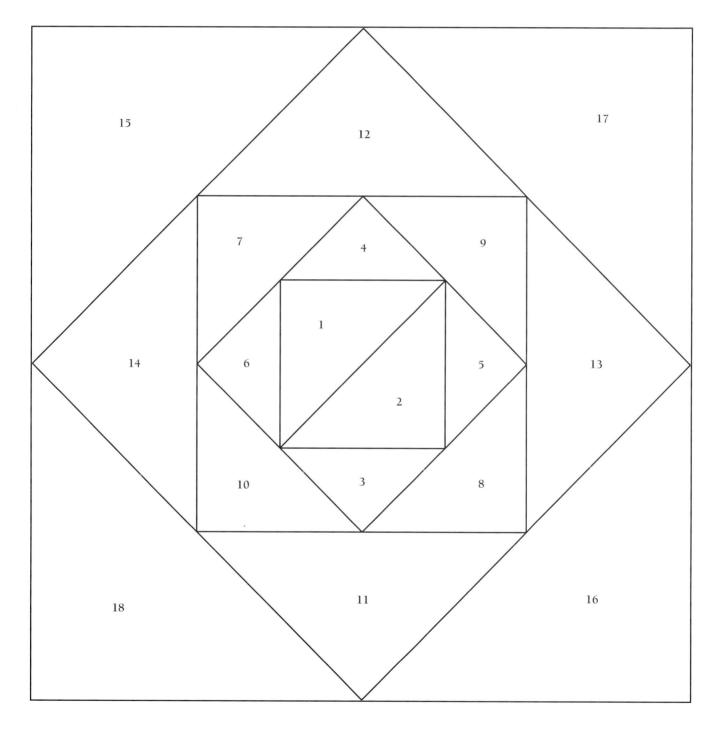

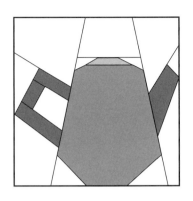

Teapot

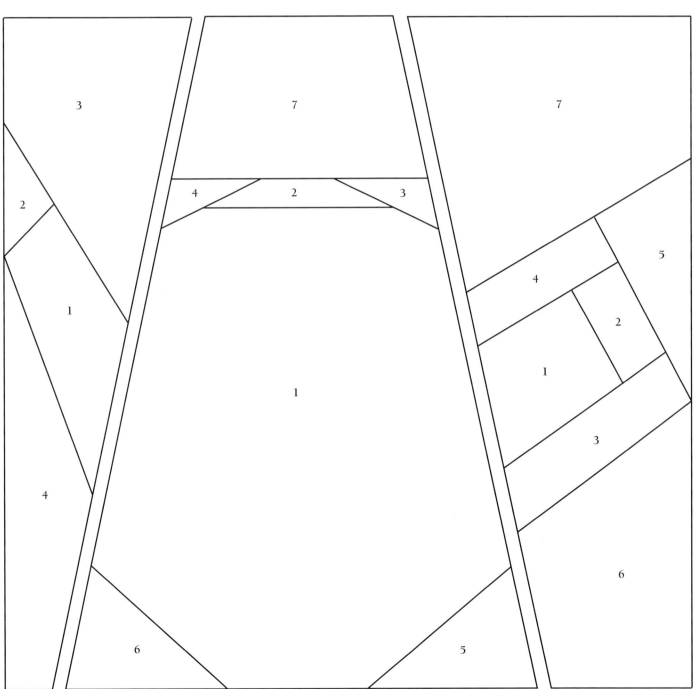

 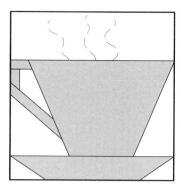

52 Cup and Saucer

Photographed block note: *Silver seed beads were sewn above cup for steam.*

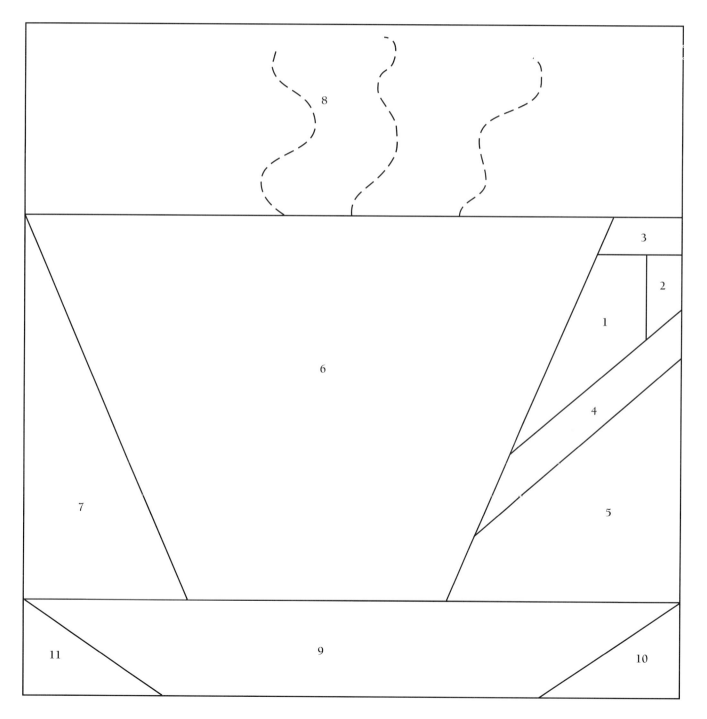

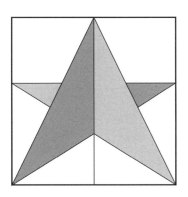

53 Five-point Star

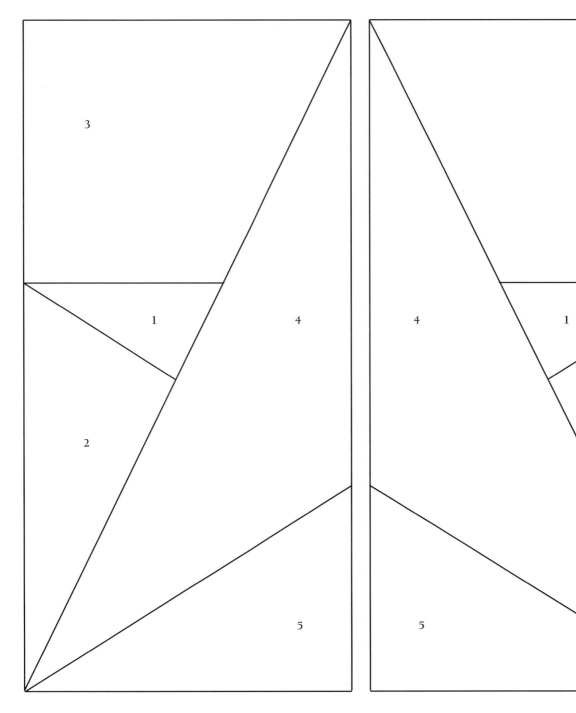

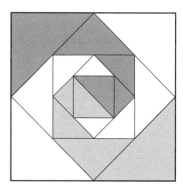

54 Snail's Trail

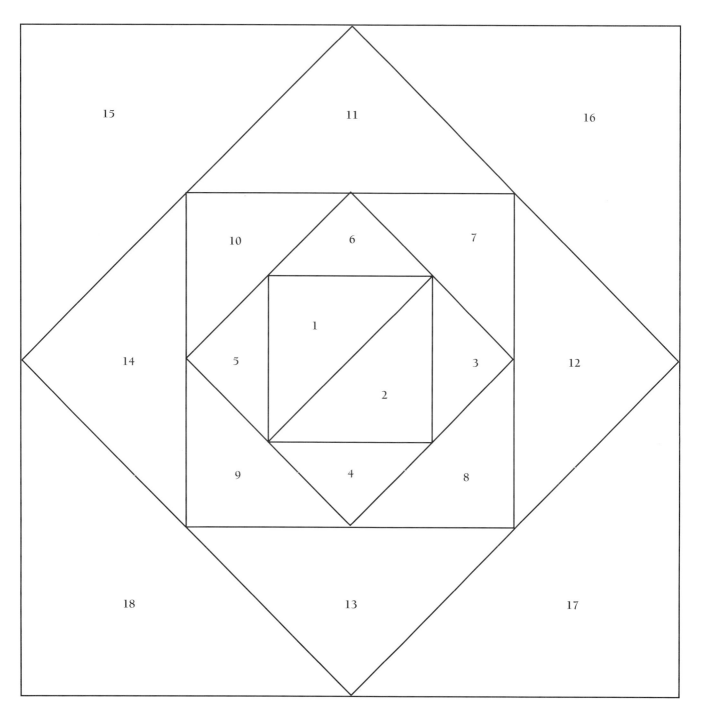

Palm Leaf

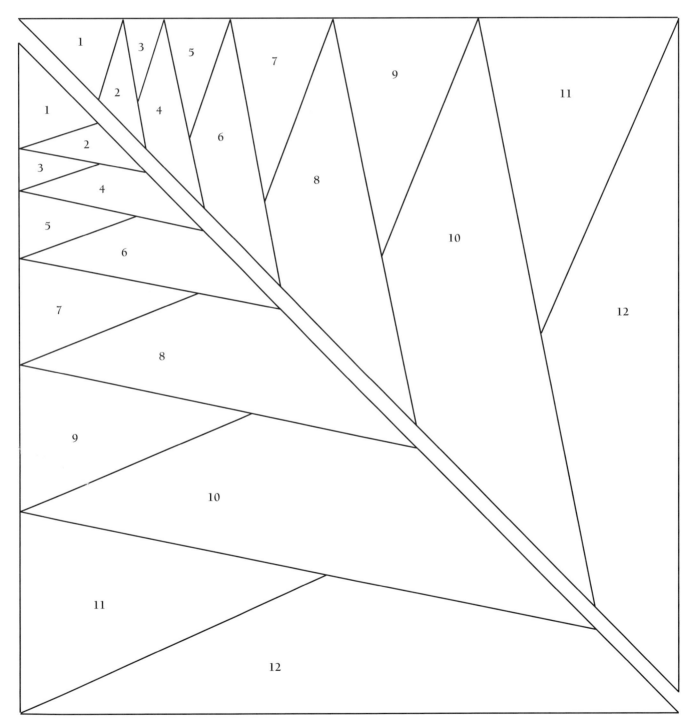

56 Bird

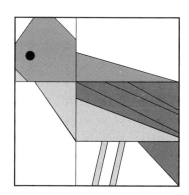

Photographed block note: *A ³/8"-diameter black button was sewn on bird's head for eye.*

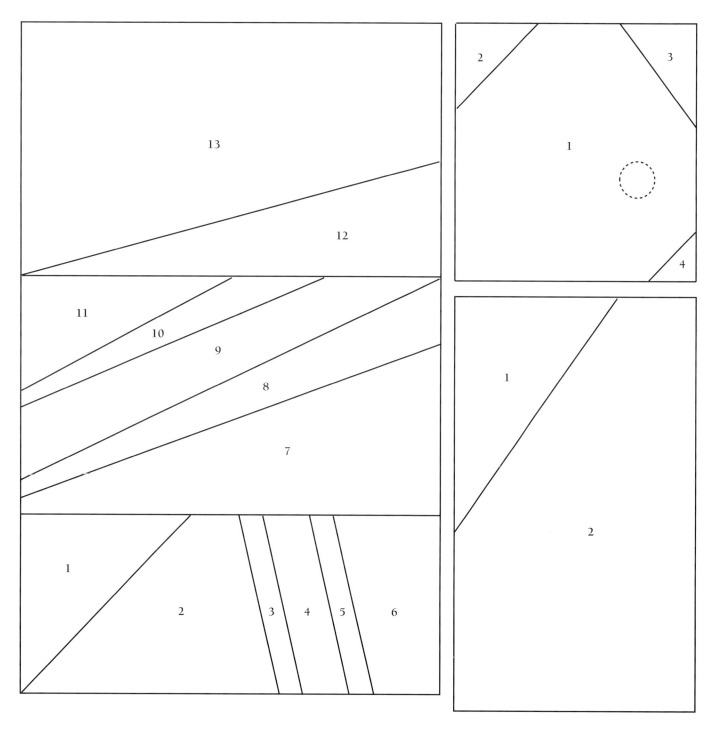

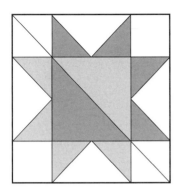

Eight-point Star

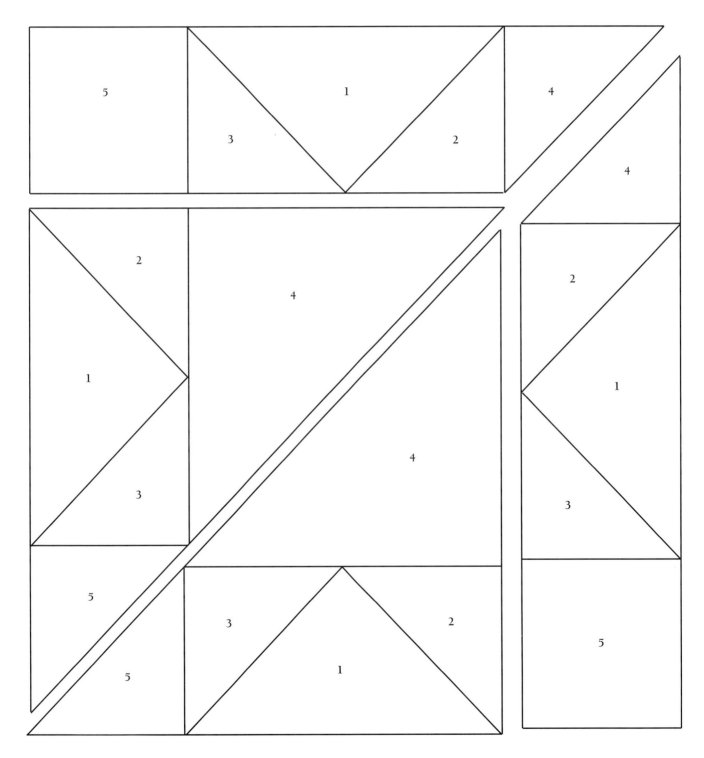

58 Pretty Pinwheel

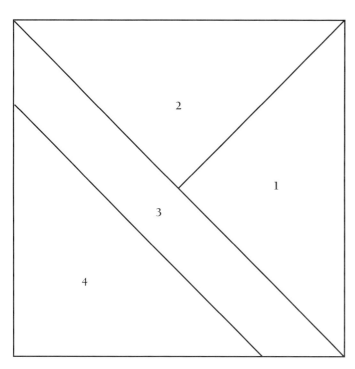

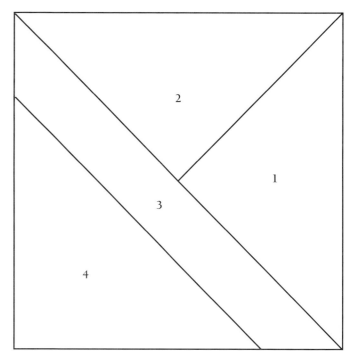

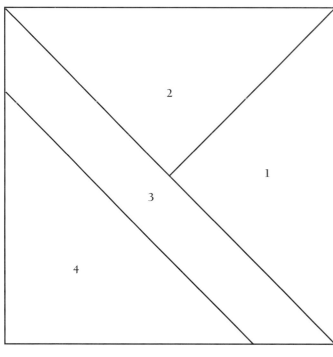

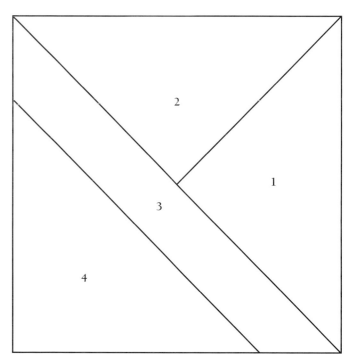

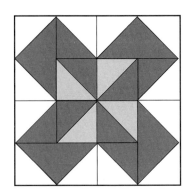

59 Pleasing Pinwheel

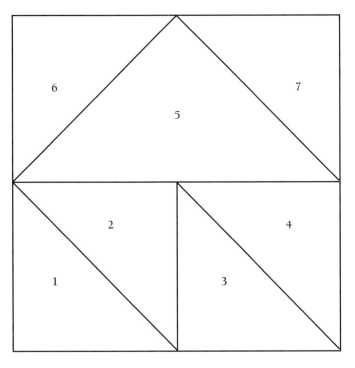

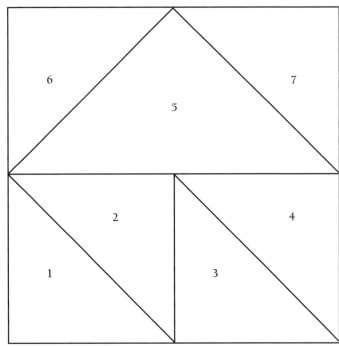

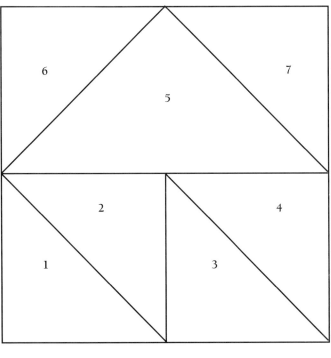

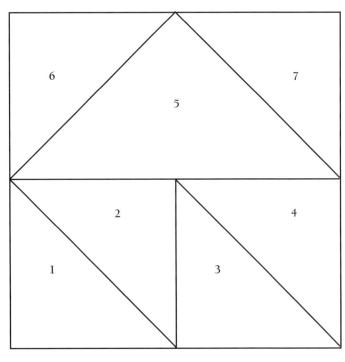

60

Geese

18	10	9	15
		8	
	6	3	
17	5	1	2	14
7		4	
		11	
19	13	12	16

Star of Bethlehem

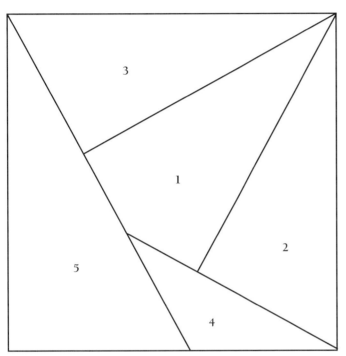

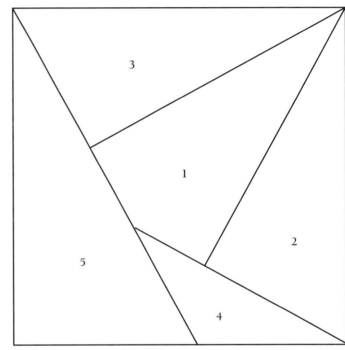

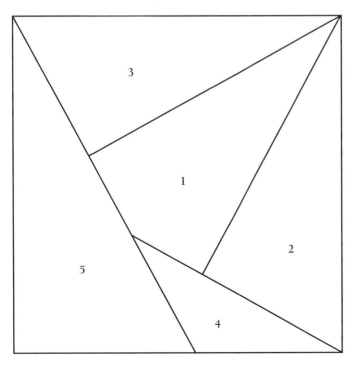

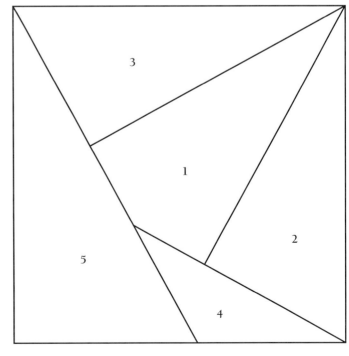

62 Lightning

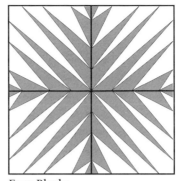

Four Blocks

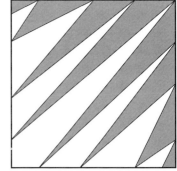

One Block

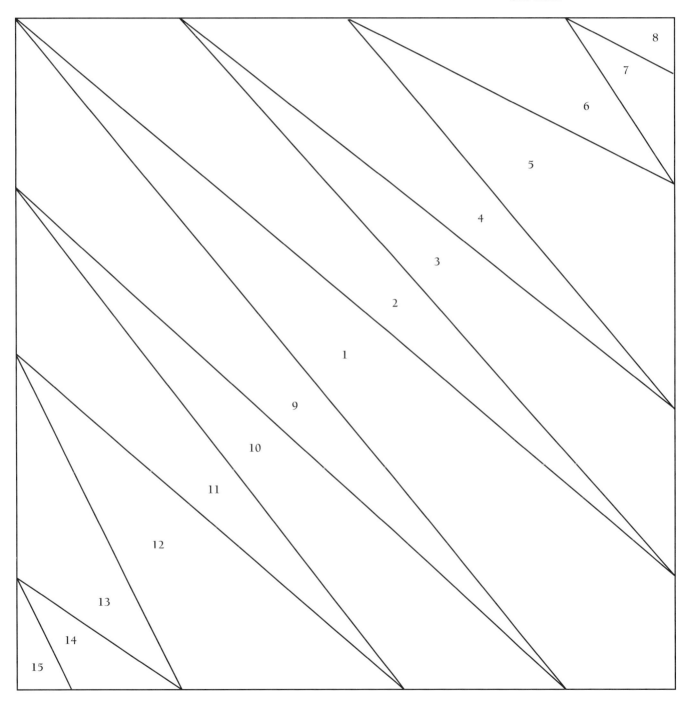

Four Blocks

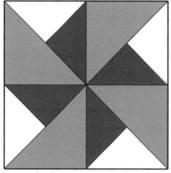
One Block

63 Pinwheel

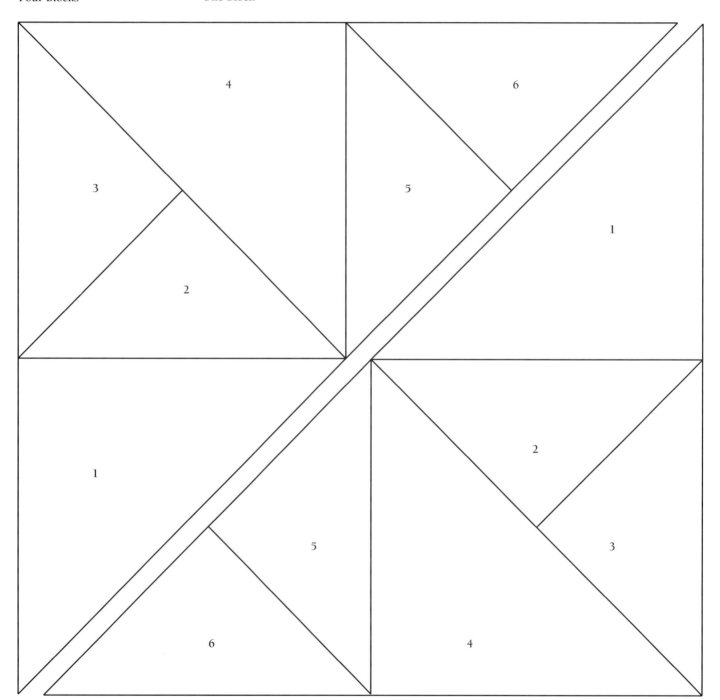

64 Kaleidoscope

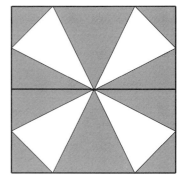
Four Blocks

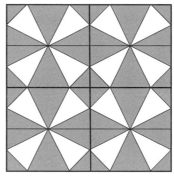
One Block

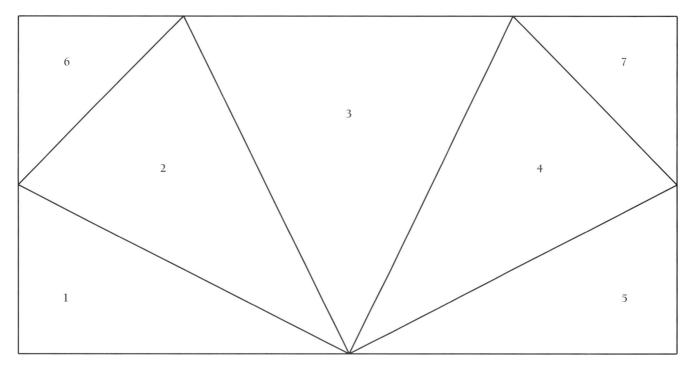

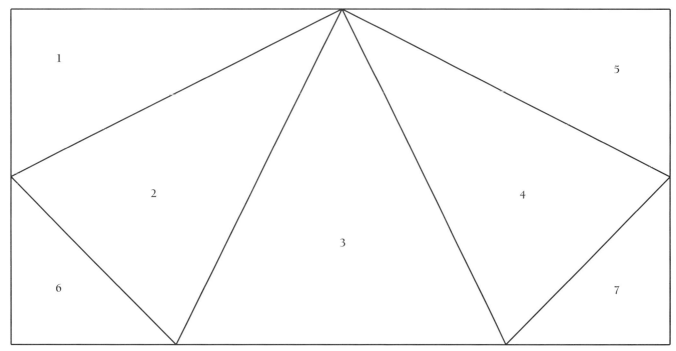

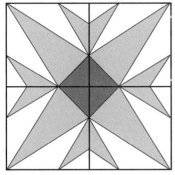
Four Blocks

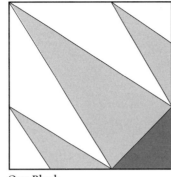
One Block

65 Star Points

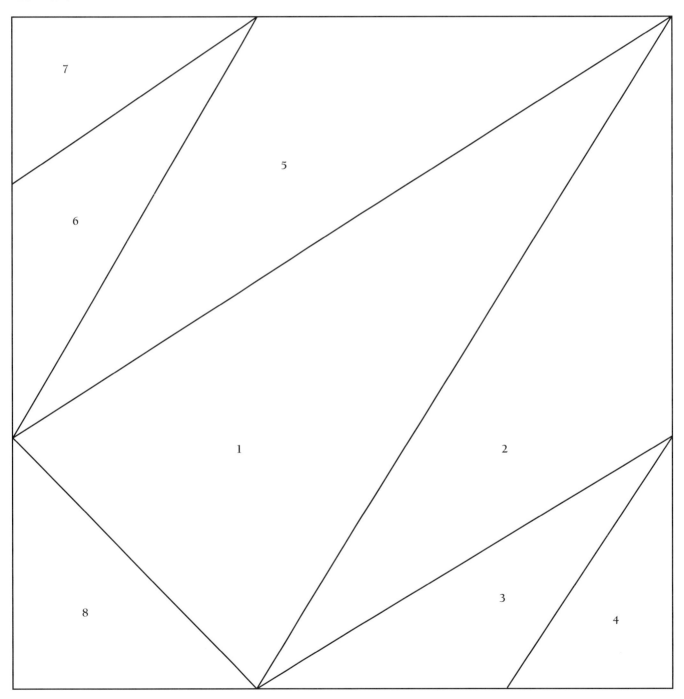

Star Award

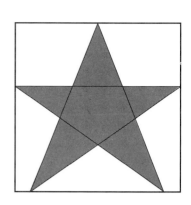

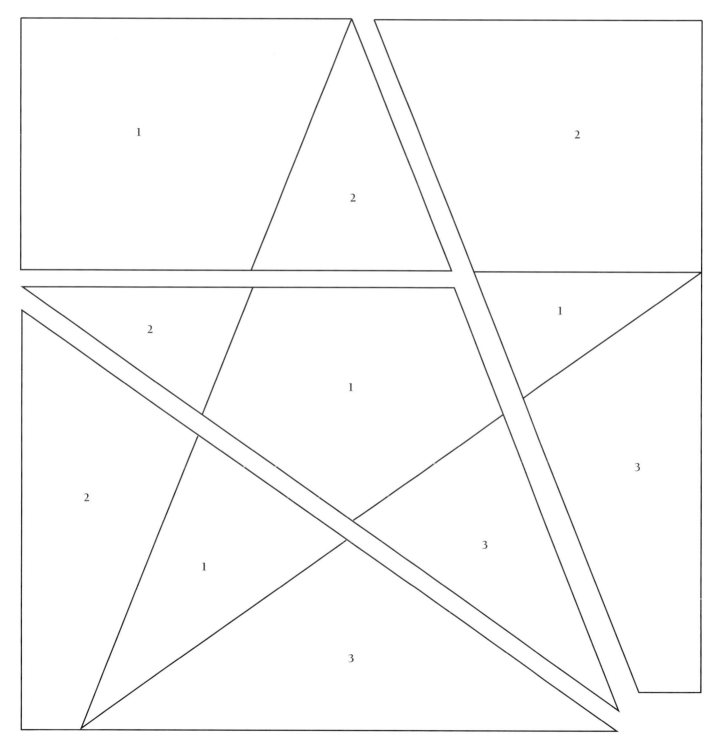

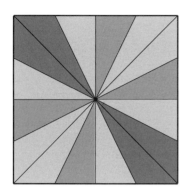

67 Spider Web

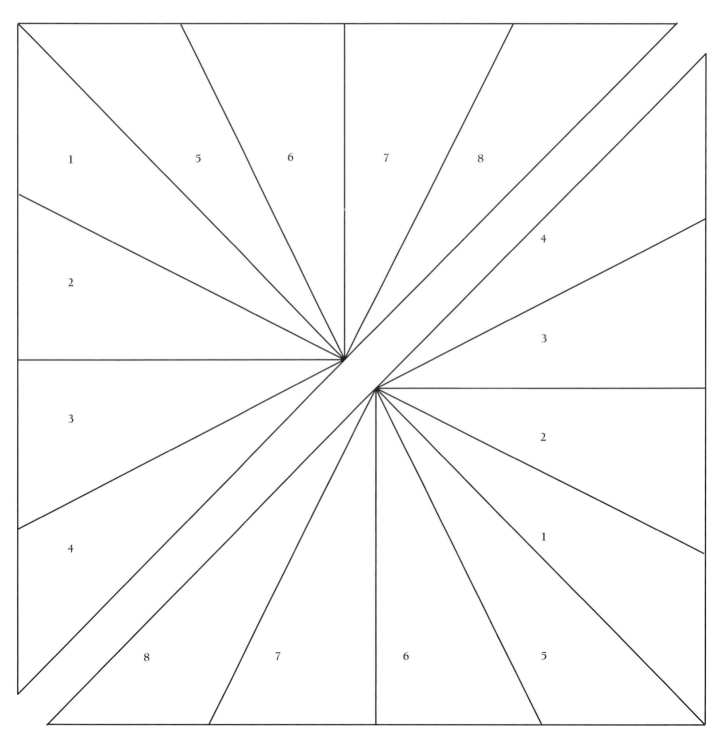

68 Log Cabin Angel

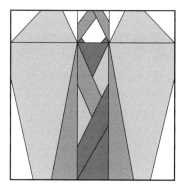

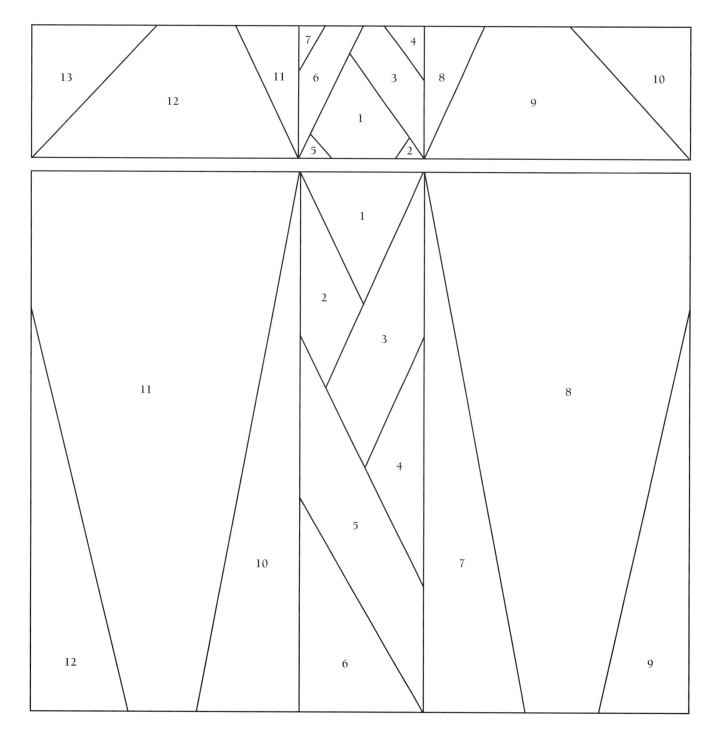

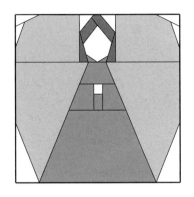

69 Celestial Angel

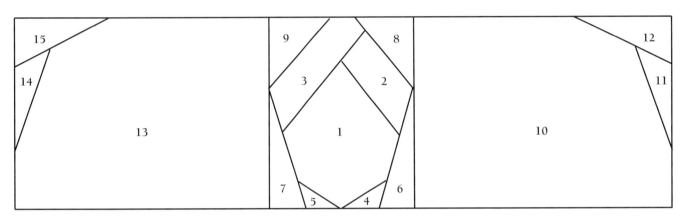

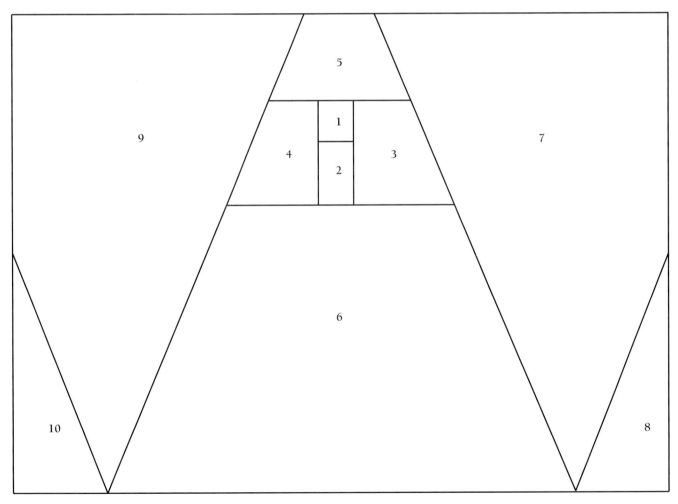

 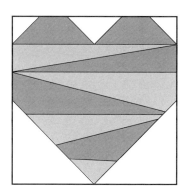

Crazy Heart

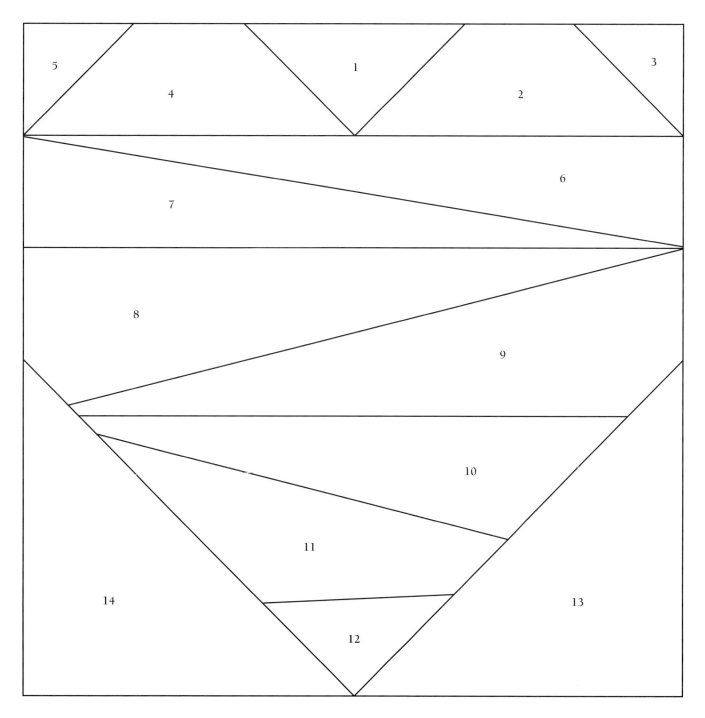

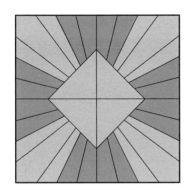

71 Sun Rays

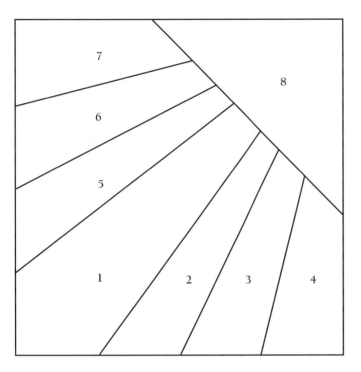

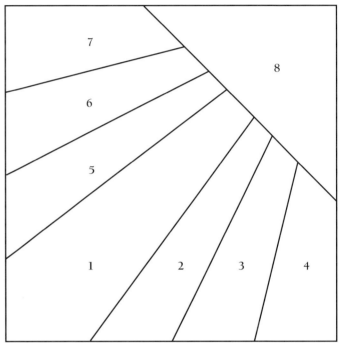

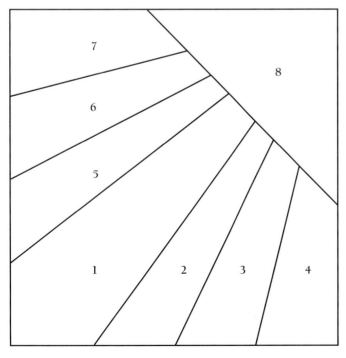

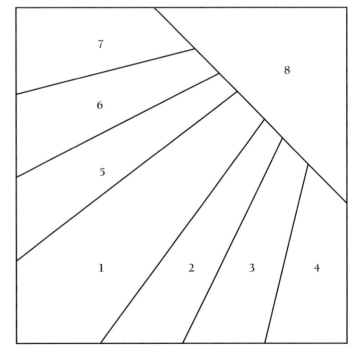

 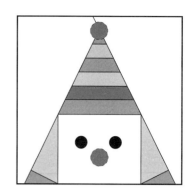

Clown

Photographed block note: *Two ¹/₂"-diameter black buttons were sewn on face for eyes; ³/₄" red pompon was tacked to face for nose and ³/₄" orange pompon was tacked at tip of hat.*

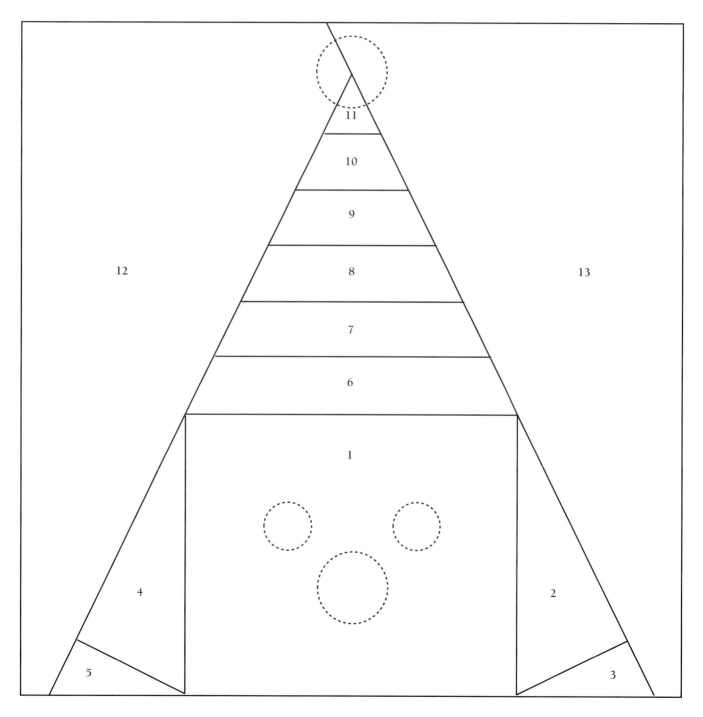

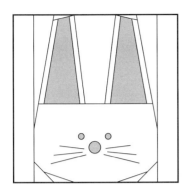

73 Bunny

Photographed block note: *Two ³/₈"-square blue buttons were sewn on bunny for eyes; one ⁵/₈" pink pompon was tacked to bunny for nose; and whiskers were hand embroidered with gray floss.*

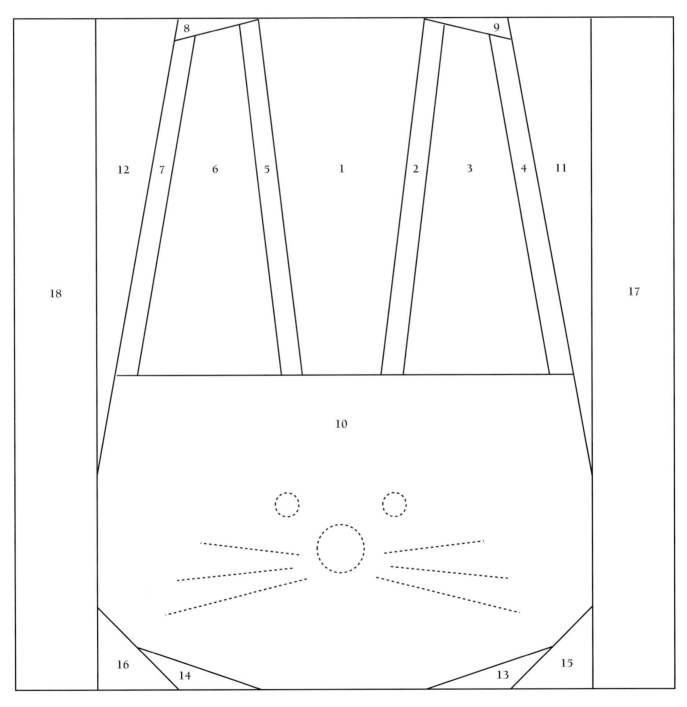

Bell

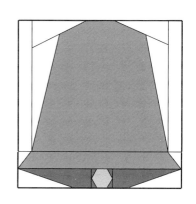

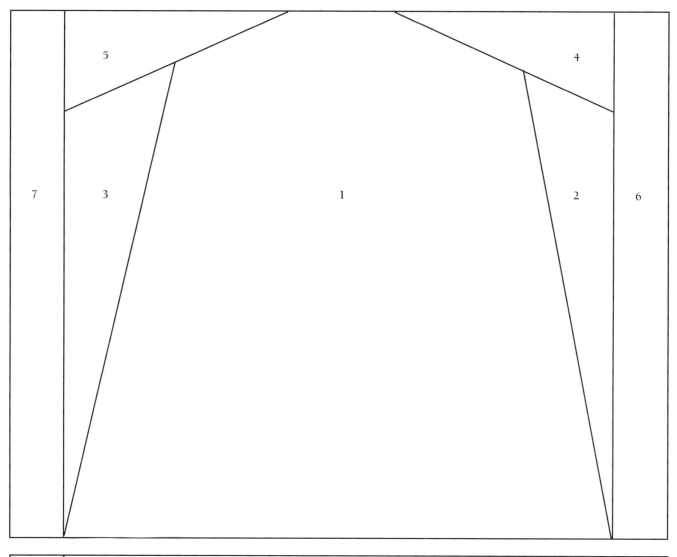

5					4	
7	3		1		2	6

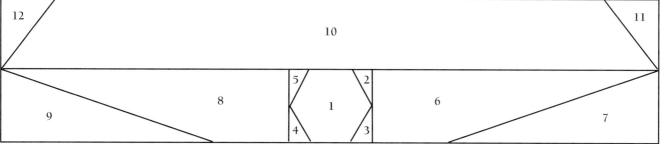

12		10		11
	5	2		
8	1		6	
9	4	3		7

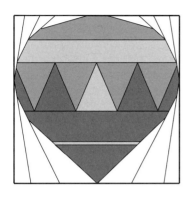

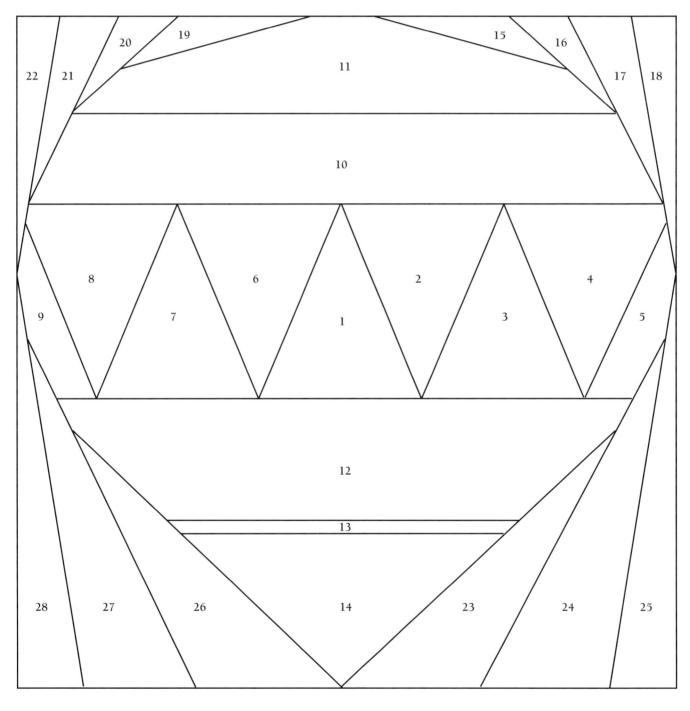

Starbright

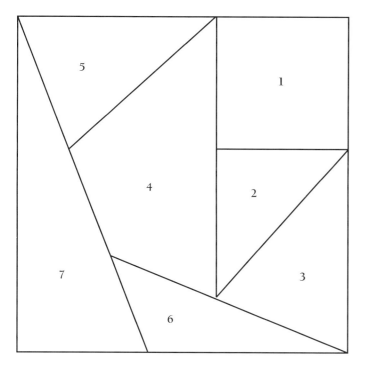

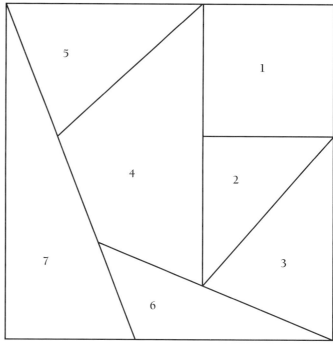

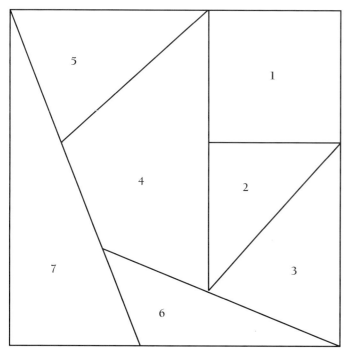

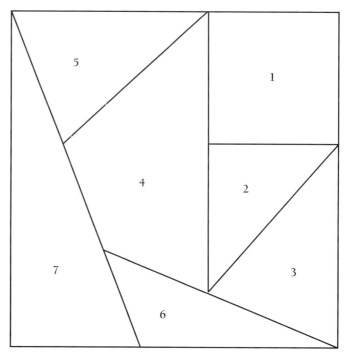

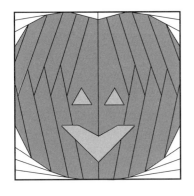

Pumpkin

Photographed block note: *Yellow felt was used for eyes and mouth.*

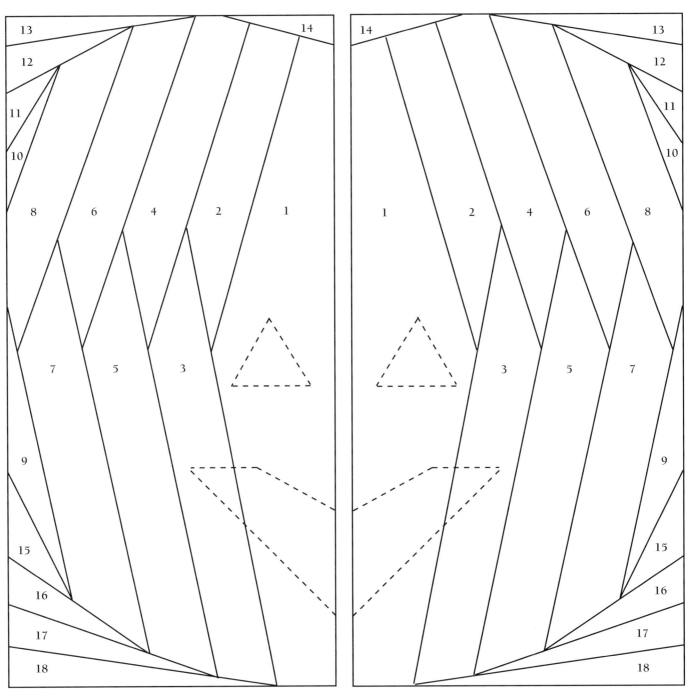

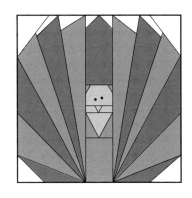

Turkey

Photographed block note: Two black seed beads were sewn to turkey's head for eyes.

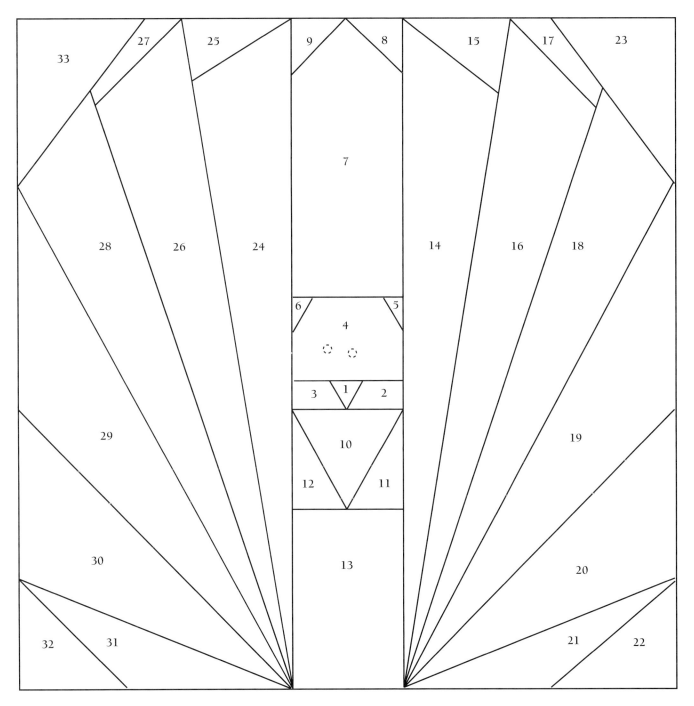

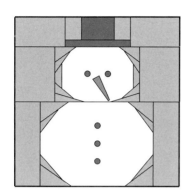

79 Snowman

Photographed block note: *Five ³/₈"-diameter buttons were sewn on snowman for eyes and buttons and a 1¹/₄"-long carrot button was used for nose.*

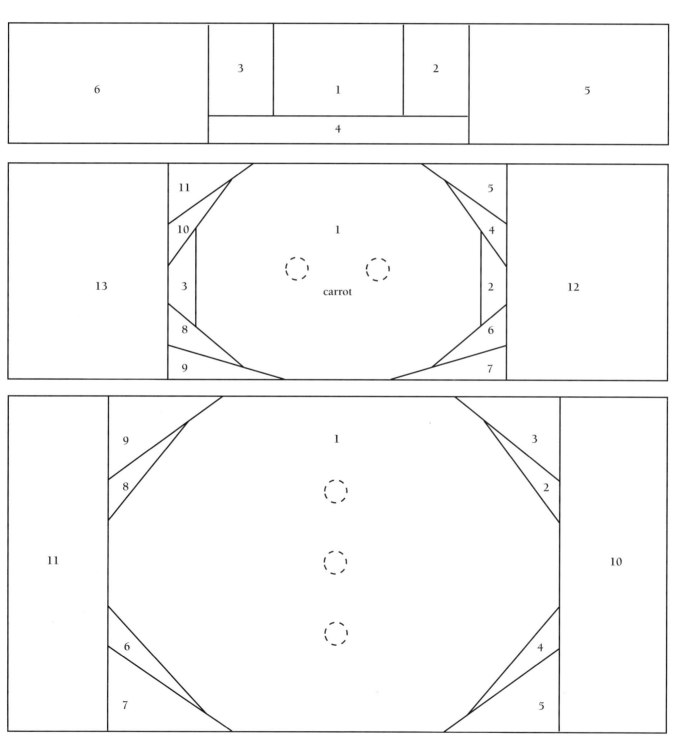

Striped Ornament

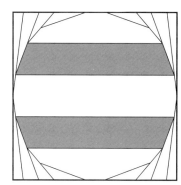

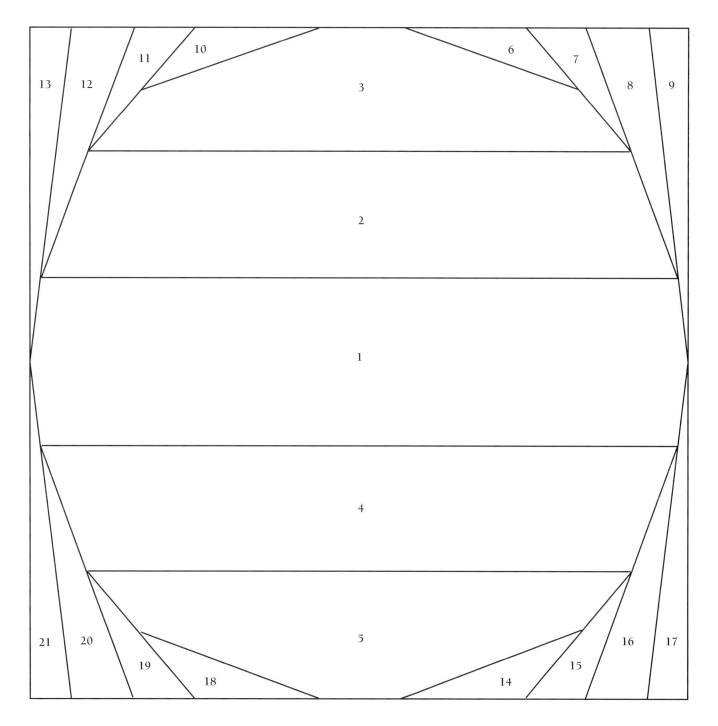

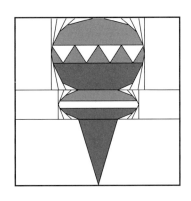

81 Elegant Ornament

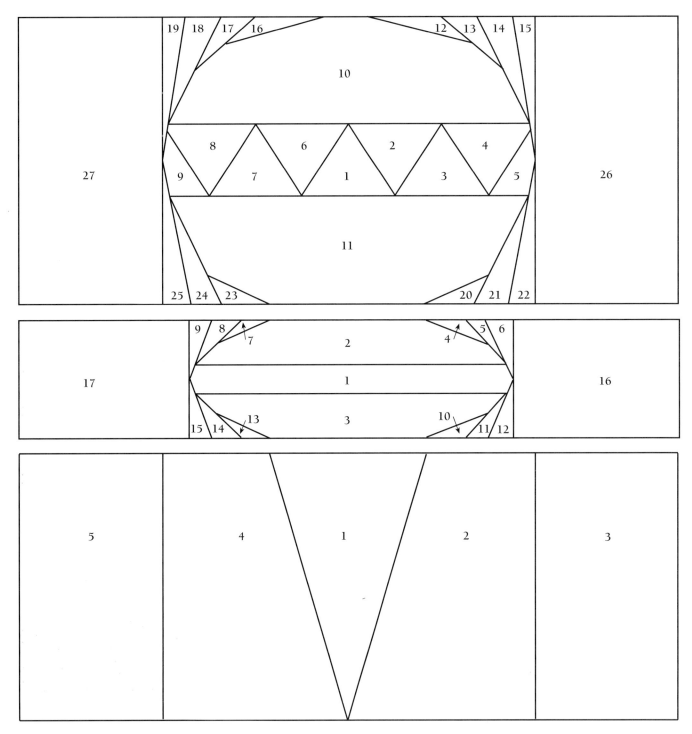

 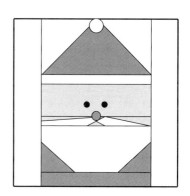

82 Santa

Photographed block note: *Two black pony beads were sewn to face for eyes; one ¹/₂" red pompon was tacked above mustache for nose; and a ³/₄" white pompon was tacked to tip of hat.*

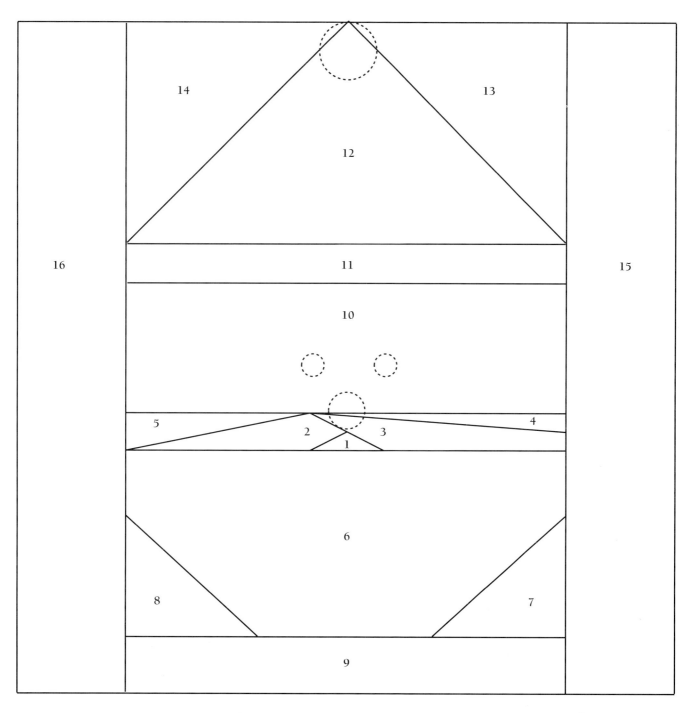

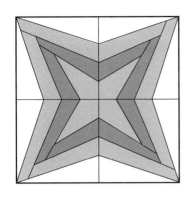

83 Starlight

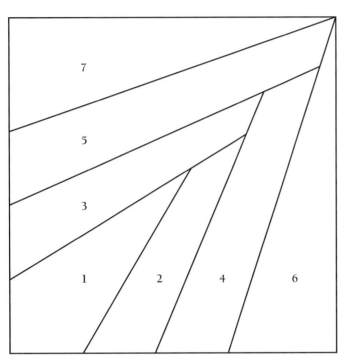

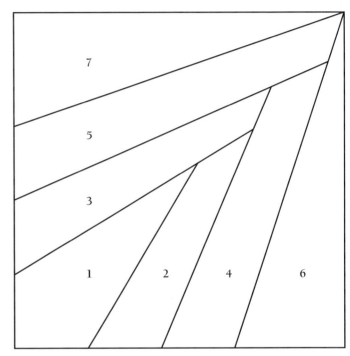

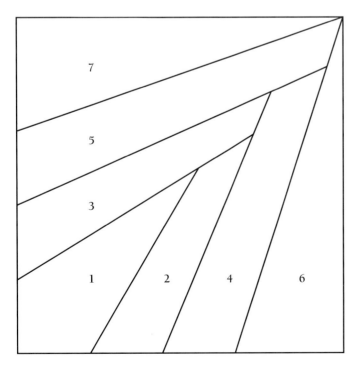

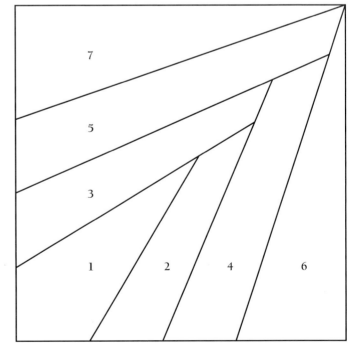

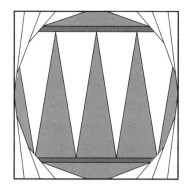

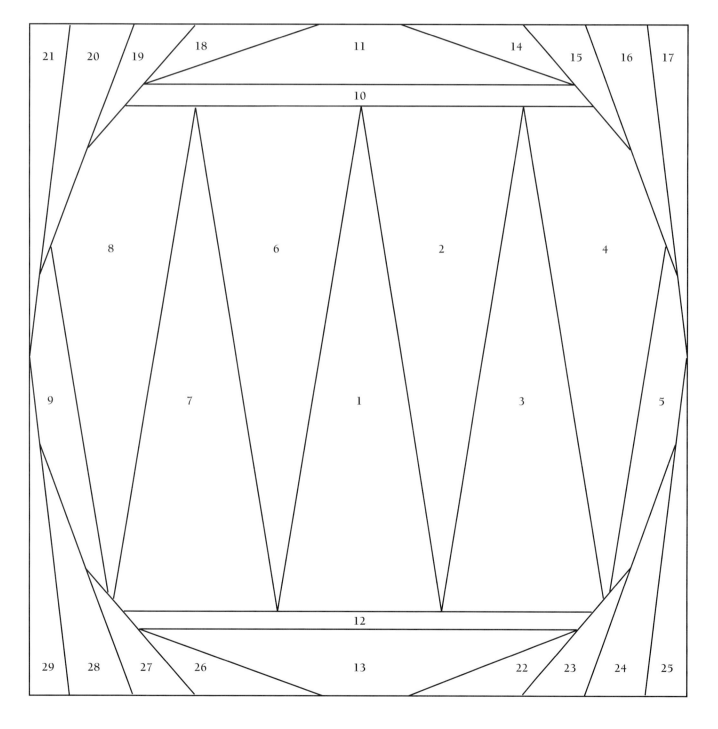

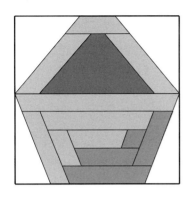

Log Cabin Basket

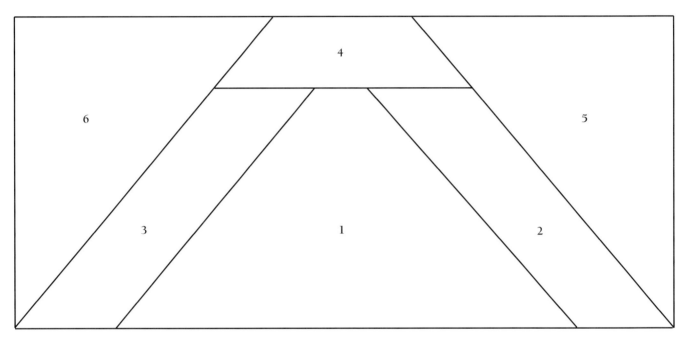

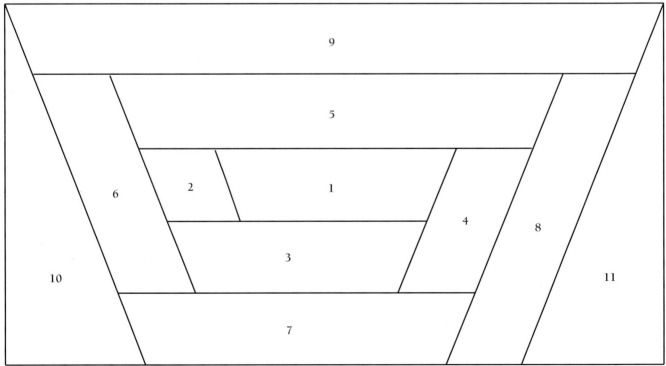

86 Flower

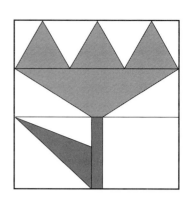

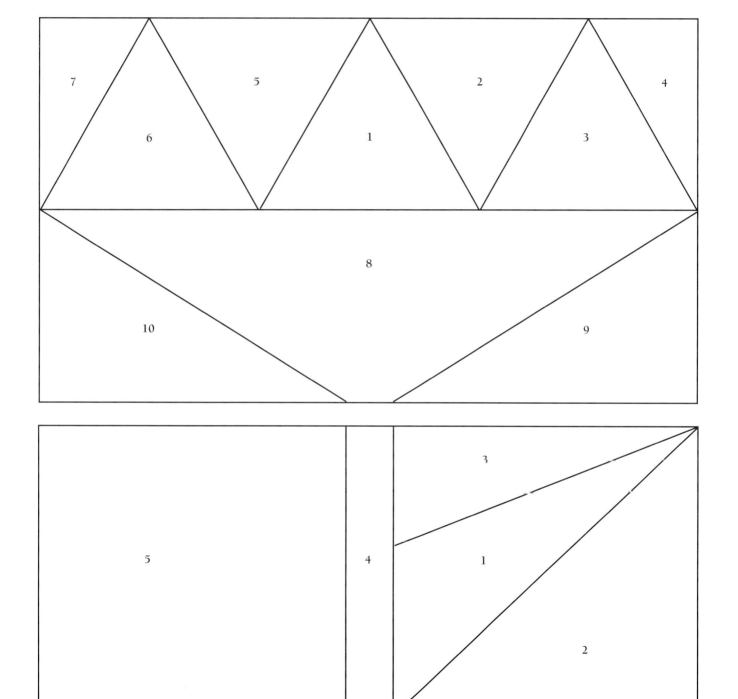

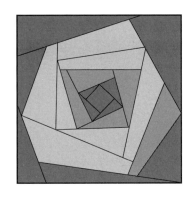

87 Crazy Rose

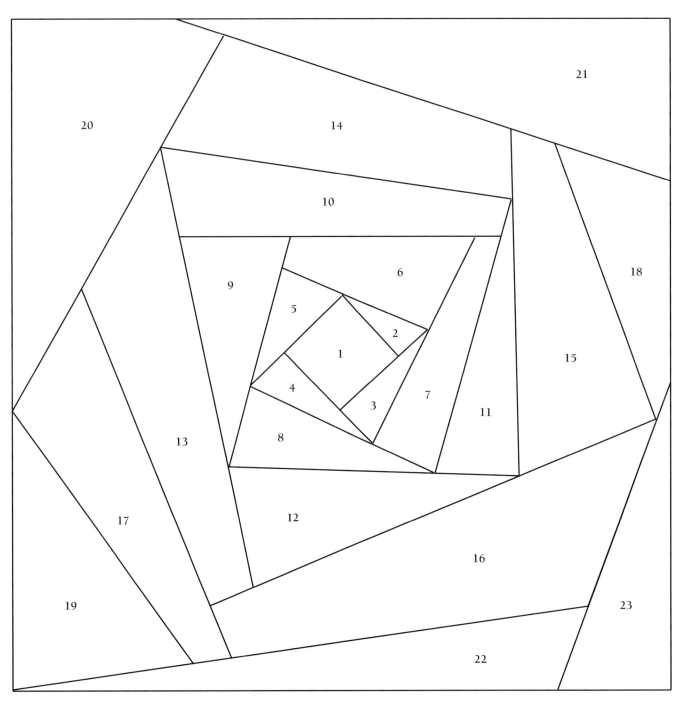

88 Log Cabin Birdhouse

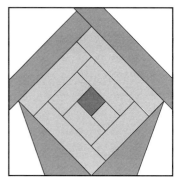

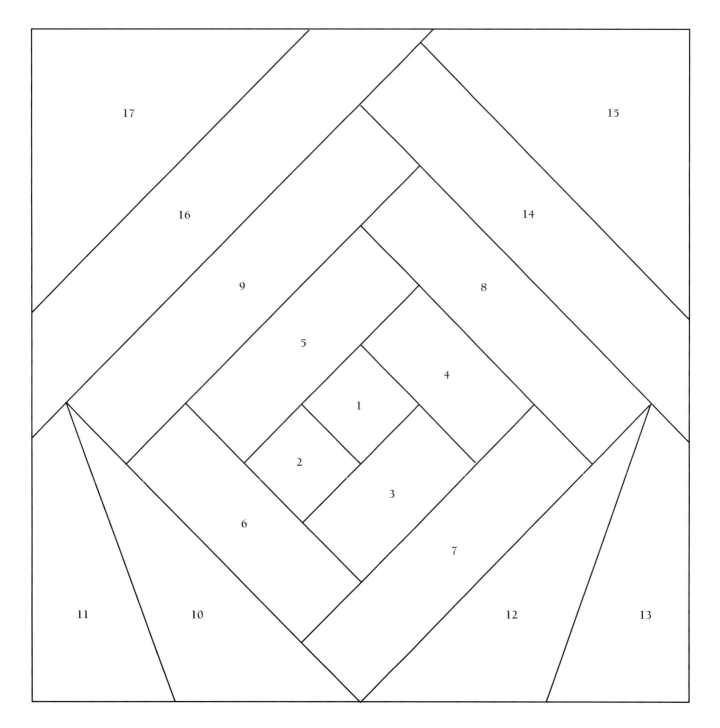

17

15

16

14

9

8

5

4

1

2

3

6

7

11

10

12

13

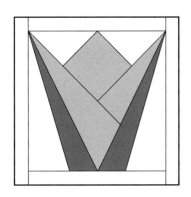

Framed Tulip

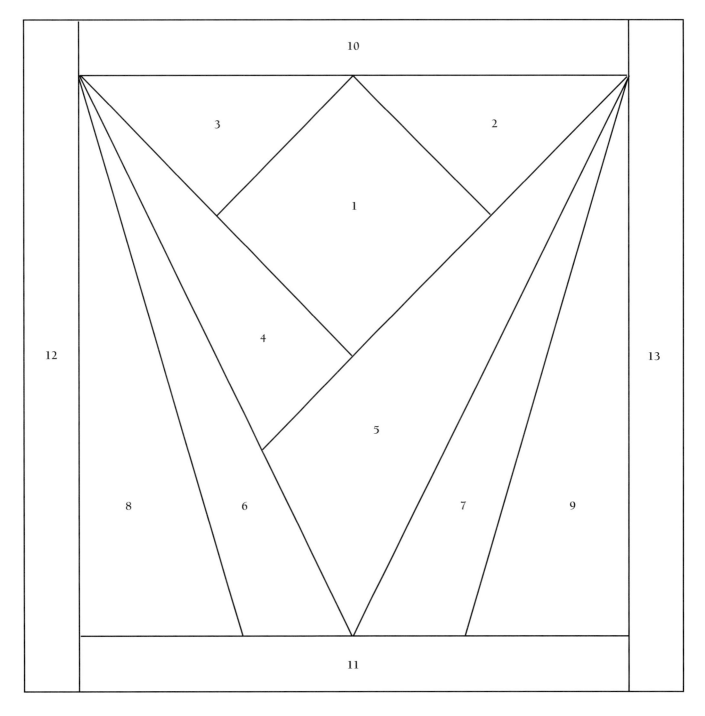

 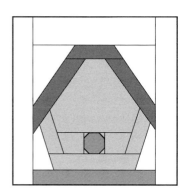

90 Bird Cottage

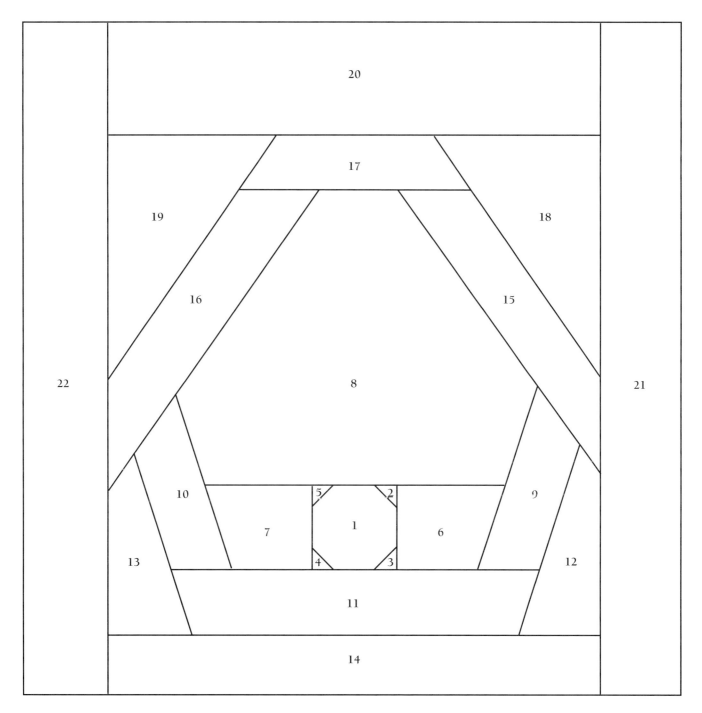

20

17

19

18

16

15

22

8

21

10

5

2

9

7

1

6

13

4

3

12

11

14

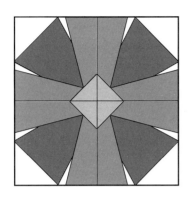

91 Blossom

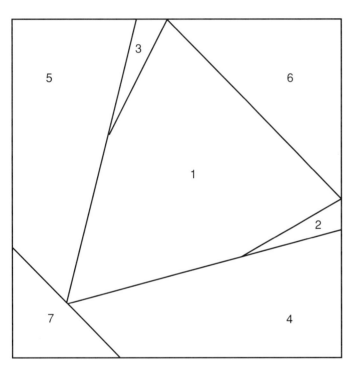

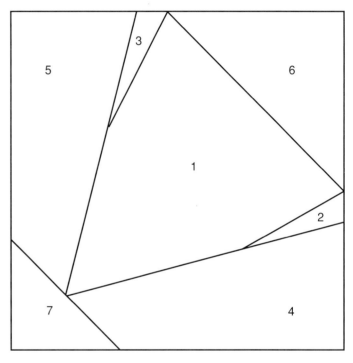

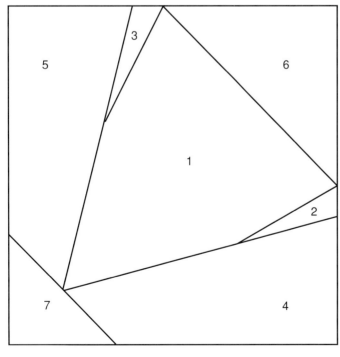

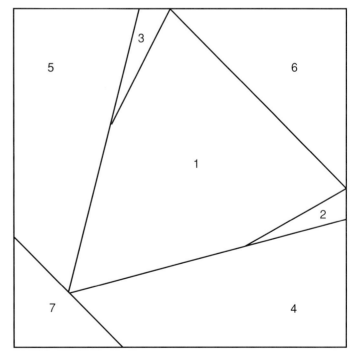

92 Tender Tulip

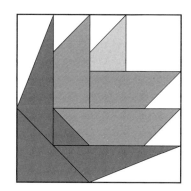

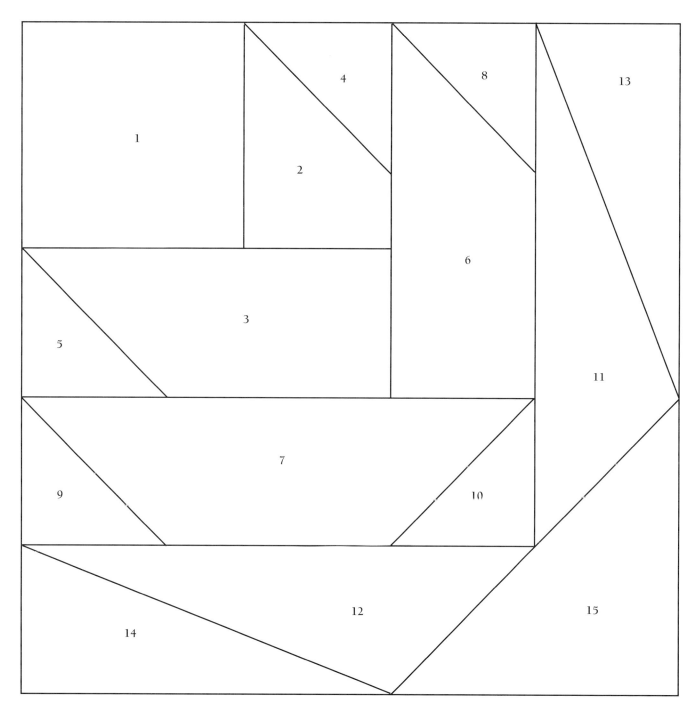

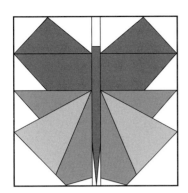

93 Butterfly Beauty

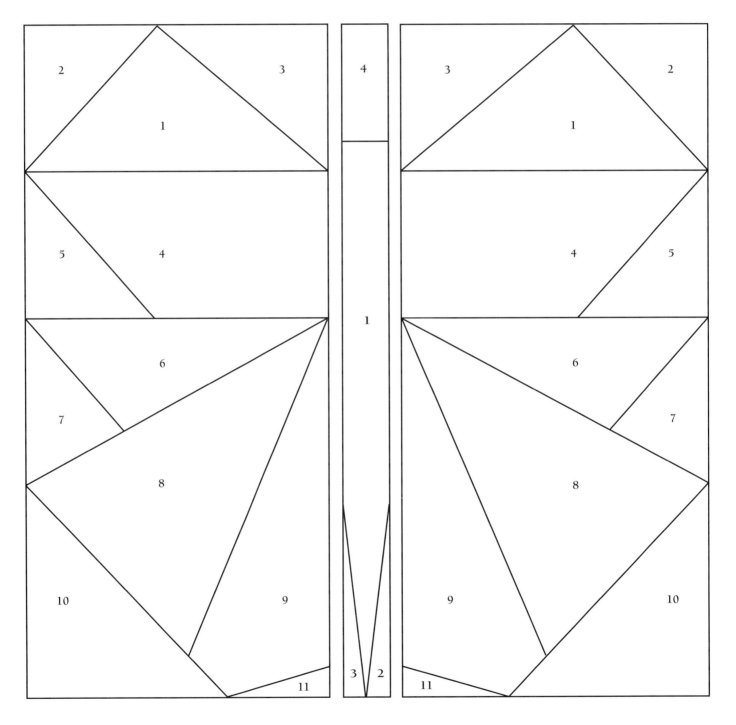

Three-story Birdhouse

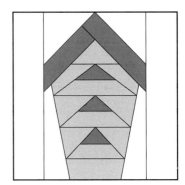

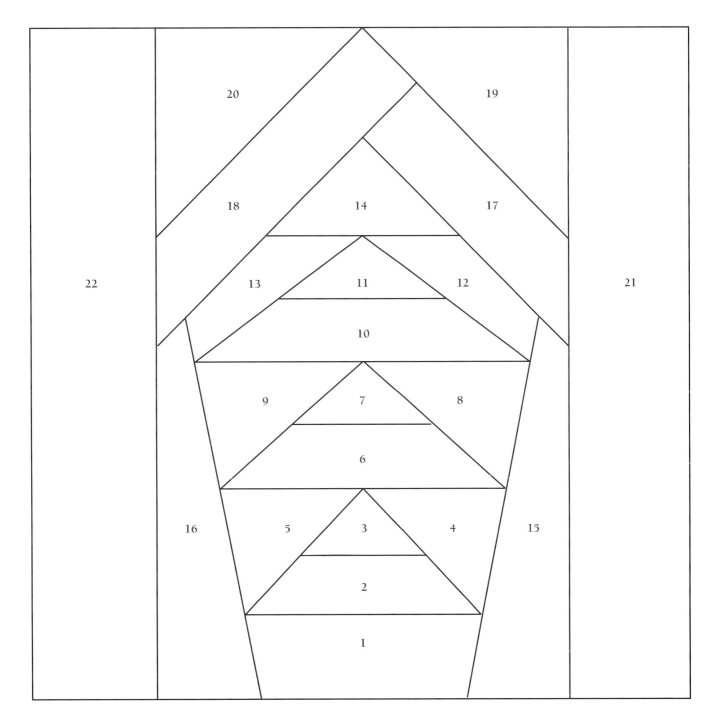

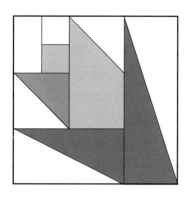

Tulip with Leaves

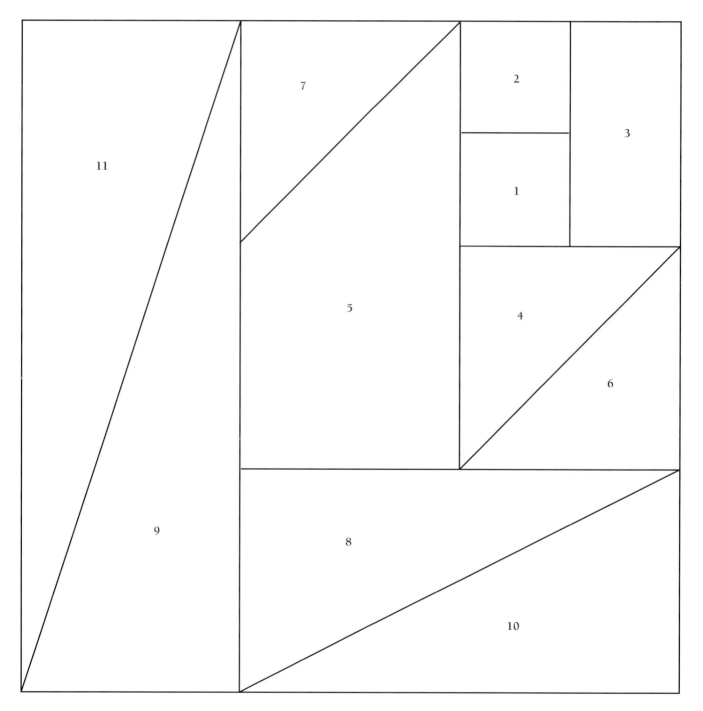

 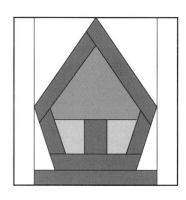

Bird Retreat

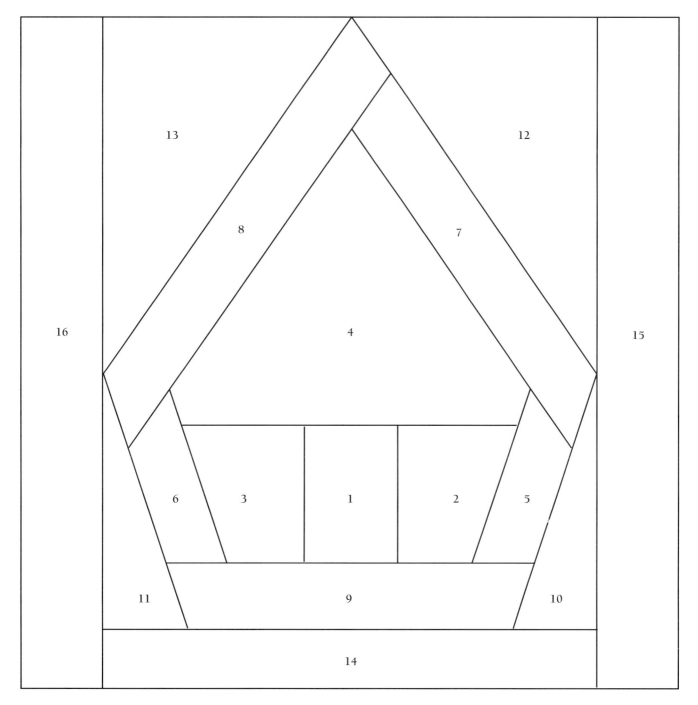

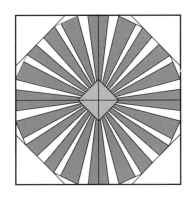

97 Bloom

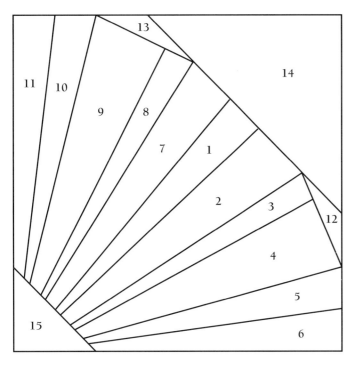

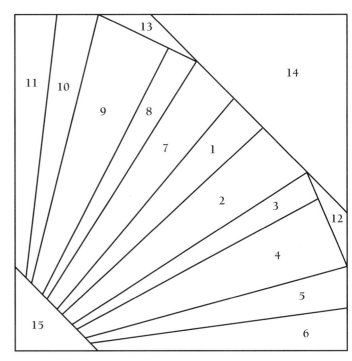

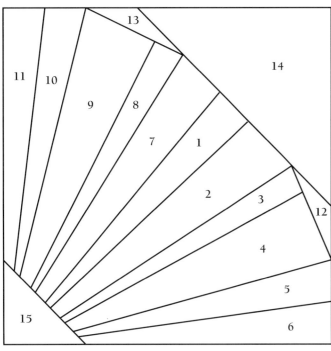

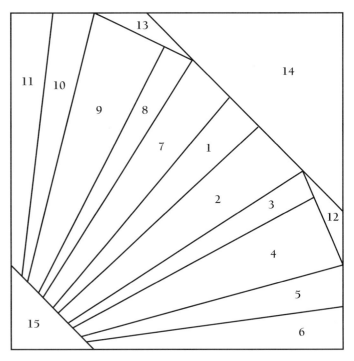

98 Bird Home

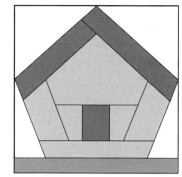

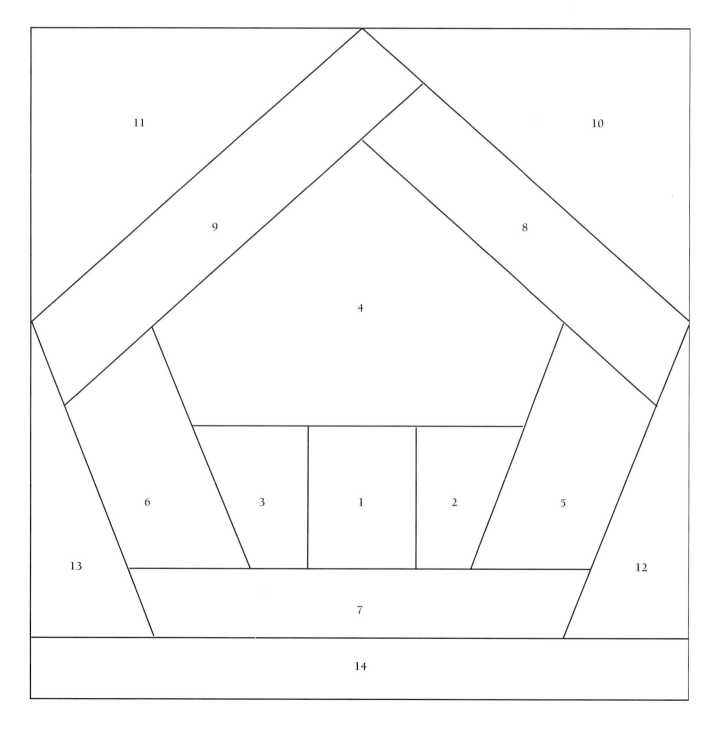

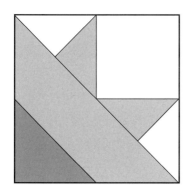

99

Tulip in Bloom

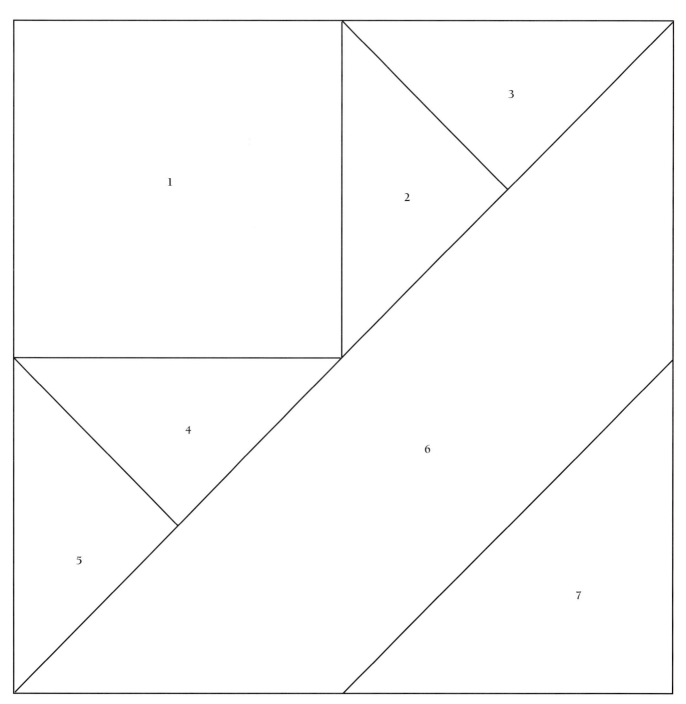

1

2

3

4

5

6

7

100

Watering Can

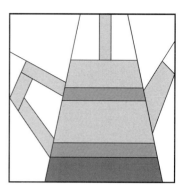

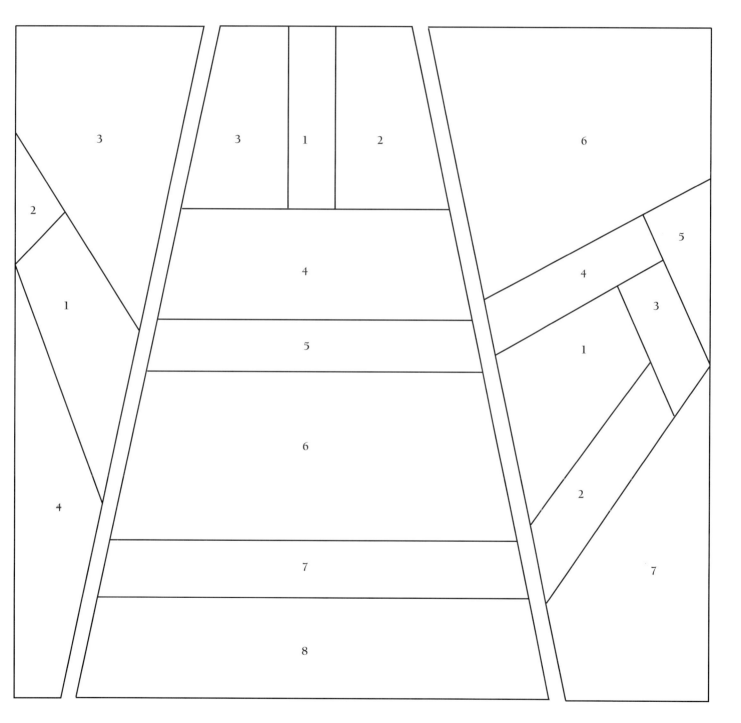

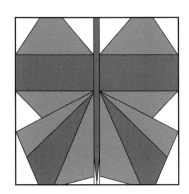

101 Brilliant Butterfly

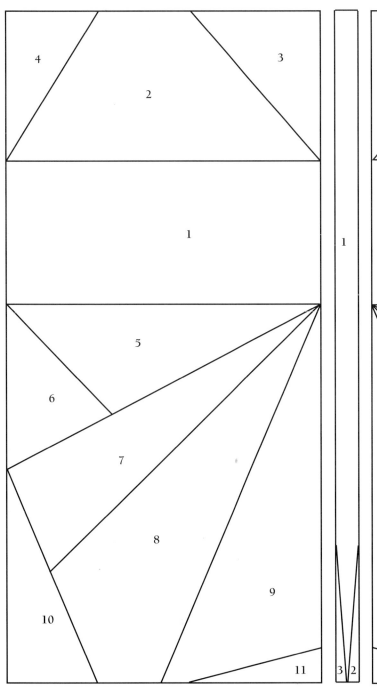

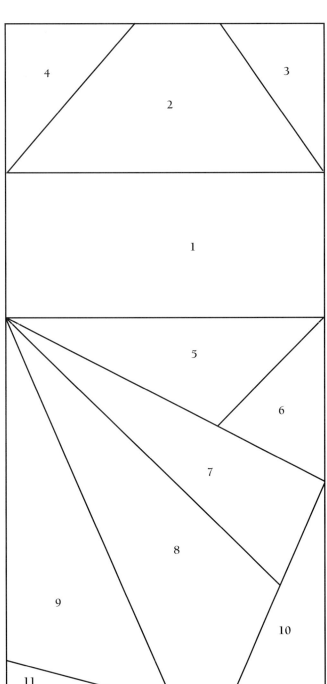